Wildfowler's Season

Books by Chris Dorsey

●

Hunt Wisconsin

The Grouse Hunter's Almanac

Pheasant Days

Game Days

Wildfowler's Season

MODERN METHODS
— for —
A CLASSIC SPORT

BY CHRIS DORSEY

Foreword by Matthew B. Connolly, Jr.

THE LYONS PRESS

Printed in Canada

Design by M.R.P. Design

10 9 8 7 6 5 4 3 2

The Library of Congress has cataloged the hardcover edition of
this work as follows:

Dorsey, Chris, 1965–
     Wildfowler's season: modern methods for a classic sport /
by Chris Dorsey; foreword by Matthew B. Connolly, Jr.
          p.   cm.
     Includes bibliographical references and index.
     ISBN 1-55821-292-2 (HC); ISBN 1-55821-714-2 (PB)
     1. Waterfowl shooting—North America.   2. Waterfowl—
North America. I. Title.
SK331.D67 1995
799.2'44'097—dc20   95-19610
                                                                      CIP

For Trevor, Matthew, Kevin, Patrick, and Tommy—
may your generation be kinder to the land than your father's.

Contents

Acknowledgments

No one writes a book alone, and many people are in one way or another a part of this project. What follows is a mere sampling of those who helped shape the character of these pages. The talents of photographers Scott Nielsen, Len Rue, Lon Lauber, Scott Liles, Charlie Heidecker, Arthur Morris, and John Hyde were especially integral in making this effort a success. Diane Jolie, *Ducks Unlimited* magazine's photo editor, helped me locate pictures of the continent's most obscure waterfowl species.

Perhaps the most rewarding part of creating this book was meeting many colorful and interesting characters who fall under the heading of "waterfowler." Scores of champion callers, amenable guides, patient friends, and innocent bystanders sacrificed hunting time so that I could preserve elements of waterfowling on film; some might even invite me back if I promise to leave my cameras at home.

Waterfowling historian Howard Harlan generously shared his wealth of information about the roots of American wildfowling, helping me present an accurate picture of our rich waterfowling legacy. The many assistants who helped me at the Library of Congress proved that some things in Washington still work. Carla Mattson at Maryland's Havre de Grace Decoy Museum gave freely of her time, sharing the museum's collection of historic waterfowling photographs. Dick McCabe at the Wildlife Management Institute proved a blessing by providing portraits of some of the legends of American conservation, people whose efforts have made a difference.

Many of my colleagues at Ducks Unlimited answered questions and shared a wealth of information that was critical throughout the formative stages of this book. Several of Ducks Unlimited's seasoned biologists helped me separate fact from fiction about our wildfowl species. To all of them, I tip my hat in gratitude.

Old friend Chuck Petrie, with whom I've shared blinds from Alaska to Texas—and one of these days he might even give me the first shot—always provided sage advice on developing the book. Favorite hunting partner Keith Gilbertson—whose diplomatic skills helped convince scores of southern Wisconsin farmers to let us hunt their duck-laden marshes—was my accomplice on many memorable field outings.

Many call, decoy, boat, and other sporting manufacturers and waterfowlers shared their facts and theories on wildfowling, information gleaned from generations of firsthand field experience. Several dedicated people at the U.S. Fish & Wildlife Service assisted in many ways, supplying illustrations and charts that are invaluable references for any waterfowler with more than a seasonal interest in wildfowl.

Jeff Howard, Janean Marti, and Barbara Krieger, champions of rare retrieving breeds, supplied snapshots of their favorite dogs—pictures seemingly as rare as those of unicorns. After much bribery and begging, many culinary wizards around the world who have treated me to unforgettable duck and goose dinners disclosed their secret recipes.

There are others whose names I do not even know. The South Dakota rancher, for instance, whose mongrel dog found my wounded goose that sailed into the abyss of a standing cornfield. It was the same dog I had chided only a few minutes earlier; no hard feelings, Champ. There was also a widowed country storekeeper in Minnesota who gave me a box of her late husband's leftover steel 2s so that I wouldn't lose a morning of hunting. There are many more who sit beside me in the blind in spirit if not in person, and thoughts of friends—past and present—lure me to favorite haunts as much as do the birds themselves.

Foreword

Perhaps it is more than the promise of wildfowl that inspires us to return year after year to favorite haunts. Maybe we revisit old blinds because we are stalking something other than birds. Thoughts of special moments in our lives—instances when a blind came to embody something more than a place to hunt—keep us company each autumn as we take our front-row seats in the wetland stages where the high drama of the annual migration is performed. As we head marshward, we take with us memories of fond days afield, places in time that we may never be able to revisit except in our thoughts.

Maybe the best duck blinds are those designed to give us a chance to think, for the periods between flights were meant for musing and for sharing the morning with a favorite blind mate—one who wouldn't hesitate to pass an easy shot so that others might enjoy the opportunity to shoot; the sort who would save his leftovers from last night's steak so that your cold, tired retriever might have more than dry kibble to eat. If you found yourself nearly out of shells, he'd hand you half of his before you'd have to ask.

But it is the birds that bring electricity to the environs to which hunters have traveled since the days when fowling pieces consisted of sticks and nets. Wildfowl are the messengers of the season, proclaiming in their hurried flights a change in the air. Just as they are living calendars, they are also daily clocks of sorts, their diurnal movements keeping time in a game as old as the wind. They bring beauty to autumn skies, for who has not marveled at their dark, inky forms silhouetted against the promise of a rising sun over an autumn marsh.

One person who knows that promise is Chris Dorsey. He has hunted waterfowl in places where most people didn't know the birds existed. From his faraway journeys to his roots in rural Wisconsin, he has accumulated a broad range of waterfowling experiences that now grace these pages. The chapters of this book represent the collective waterfowling experiences of those with whom he has shared a blind. They are people who range from world champion duck and goose callers to decoy makers, shooting experts, master retriever trainers, biologists, boatbuilders, clothing manufacturers, waterfowling historians, and wild-game chefs.

This book will introduce you to those many personalities and will become, itself, a favorite partner. It is a waterfowler's family album, linking the modern duck and goose hunter with the heritage that is uniquely the wildfowlers'.

—MATTHEW B. CONNOLLY, JR.
Executive Vice President
Ducks Unlimited, Inc.

Introduction

Imagine standing alongside a Tule Indian and his crude decoys of two thousand years ago, crouched in the reeds with a spear while waiting for a canvasback to appear from the heavens—a bird delivered by the gods of the hunt. Picture yourself peering over the shoulder of a market gunner on a starlit night on Chesapeake Bay, poised with lanterns and a 150-pound punt gun that could raze whole rafts of unsuspecting fowl. Think about sharing a blind with Nash Buckingham, watching him train his famous gun, Bo-Whoop, on a pair of high mallards. What would you give to listen to a conversation between Ding Darling and Aldo Leopold, witnessing the genesis of American waterfowl conservation?

The blood of a modern waterfowler courses with heritage, for we are ultimately the culmination of the people and events that have shaped the sport we know today. Ours is a pastime fraught with tradition, for the stories and artifacts of yesteryear survive as legends and icons of another era. Laced throughout this book are information and anecdotes connecting us to that past, celebrating the rich history and lore unique to the waterfowler. There is current information, too, for much has changed in the world of duck and goose hunting since the days of Grinnell, Leffingwell, and Bruette.

The spirit of the waterfowler, however, has not changed. Who but a wildfowler would find a blustery December day inviting? Name

Photo by Scott Nielsen, courtesy Ducks Unlimited, Inc.

another breed of hunter who would spend a morning waist deep in mud and cattails for the chance to give his retriever work. What other creature is at home in a blind built of wooden planks, cattail stems, and enthusiasm? Name someone who would risk his financial future to buy a swamp, and odds are he'll be a waterfowler.

Whether it's sunsets punctuated by the silhouettes of rising mallards, the chorus of a marsh coming to life with a sunrise, or the companionship of special people, waterfowling strikes a different chord in each of us. At the center of our attraction for the sport, however, are the birds themselves, migrants that traverse a continent annually and add drama to autumn skies. Grand ideas can be born in duck blinds, for many of America's leading conservationists found both inspiration and motivation from what they saw and felt as they awaited encounters with wildfowl. Leopold's "land ethic," Darling's determination, and Teddy Roosevelt's vision likely owe their genesis to the same wetland cathedrals that have become so important to us all.

Their legacy lives today in the community of waterfowlers, for no other sporting patronage has embraced Leopold's notion that we must be stewards of the land with the reverence of the waterfowler. Millions of acres of wetlands and other habitats have been spared development thanks to the efforts of duck and goose hunters across the continent. Having seen firsthand the wonders of wetlands, waterfowlers know what is at stake when plans call for a marsh to be surrendered to the plow or a slough to be drained for development.

This book is a celebration of the waterfowler and a tribute to the sport that has taught generations of hunters the value of marshes, picturesque dawns, and friendship afield. It is written for those who pay homage to wildfowl each autumn, for the magic in whistling wings overhead brings us back, inexorably, to the theaters of the marshlands.

*I*n the Beginning

Modern waterfowling has evolved from what was once a matter of subsistence to what is now a pursuit of sport. Enjoying the athleticism of a trained retriever as it collects a fallen bird, swinging a well-balanced shotgun, and blowing a finely tuned call are all pastimes we've come to cherish. Our predecessors, however, had a very different view of wildfowling.

While early American waterfowlers may have enjoyed their moments afield, they were inspired by two motives very different from ours: food and money. The Tule Eaters—aboriginal Americans who were the ancestors of the Northern Paiutes—probably were less concerned with the beauty of a duck-dotted sunrise than with getting dinner when they fashioned the first known duck decoys from a combination of feathers and rushes, creations clearly resembling canvasbacks. One was discovered in Lovelock Cave, Nevada, in 1924, estimated to date from A.D. 800. Archaeologists speculate, however, that waterfowl decoys could have been in use as much as eight thousand years earlier.

Other early American Indians and white settlers of the 1600s used decoys of much less sophistication, as simple as small piles of kelp and seaweed, bird skins stuffed with grass, and even collections of stones. Ducks and geese were plentiful and, as one might imagine, easily fooled compared with today's heavily hunted waterfowl.

This 1910 photo depicts a pair of market gunners standing with their daily take in front of A. C. Ward's general store in Norfolk, Virginia's Market Place. Courtesy Bill Walsh.

Live ducks and geese and carved wooden blocks ultimately replaced these crude early decoys. American sporting magazines of the late nineteenth century detailed methods to train live decoys, and many gunning clubs of the period kept flocks of beguiling ducks and geese at their estates for use as decoys. George Bird Grinnell, in *American Duck Shooting*, wrote about the era of the live decoys: "At Silver Lake, in Massachusetts, the various clubs possess hundreds of live goose decoys, of which a large proportion are so well trained that they are thrown into the air."

As effective as they were, live decoys were not practical for the market gunners of the East Coast tidewaters, who required large numbers of easily manageable "stool," a term referring to the old European practice of fastening a live pigeon to a pole or perch to lure other pigeons. The market hunters of yesteryear are often ridiculed for their excesses, but although they were ruthless killers, they were also remarkably inventive, continually pioneering hunting methods to increase their take and, ultimately, their profits. Reviewing a list of famous early decoy carvers is akin to reading a who's who of market gunners, for the two were inseparable. Market gunners often used huge numbers of decoys—sometimes as many as five hundred in a spread—to concentrate flocks of ducks for efficient killing. By the early 1800s, rough decoys carved primarily of white cedar were commonly used by notable market gunners, who grew increasingly proficient in their slaughter of wildfowl. The term "blocks," often used to describe decoys, originates from the crude forms of these early decoys.

In the fabled waterfowling areas of the Chesapeake Bay, the largest inland body of water on the Atlantic Coast, stretching 170 miles from the Virginia Capes to the Susquehanna Flats and comprising some four thousand miles of shoreline, huge muzzleloading guns—commonly larger than 4 gauge and often homemade—exacted heavy tolls on ducks, brant, and geese. Upward of one hundred ducks might be taken with a single shot from one of these cannons, which sometimes weighed in excess of 150 pounds. When loaded with two pounds of shot and several ounces of powder, the effect was devastating. "The big guns fired a huge pattern, centering on the swimming ducks but often killing birds flying twenty feet in the air," reported David and Jim Kimball in their book, *The Market Hunter*.

Tidewater market gunners favored canvasbacks over other species. There are two accounts as to how the birds derived their com-

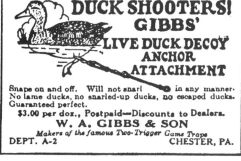

These two advertisements selling leg straps to use with live decoys appeared in the September 1928 issue of National Sportsman. The practice of using live decoys was banned nationwide in 1935.

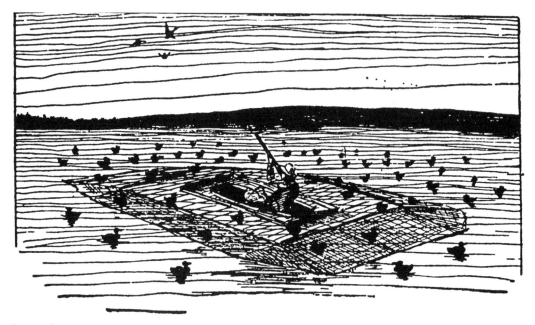

Illustration from American Duck, Goose & Brant Shooting, *1929.*

mon name: The first is that they were often shipped to market in canvas sacks—hence, the name canvasback. The second, and perhaps more likely, stems from the canvaslike pattern found on the ducks' backs. The Chesapeake Bay was once rich with wild celery, the favorite food of canvasbacks, and the ducks were both plentiful and easy to kill. Couple that with the fact that they were also the choice fowl of eastern gastronomes, and you have the ingredients for decimation. Fine restaurants in most major eastern cities offered wildfowl on their menus by about 1850. Grinnell wrote that upward of fifteen thousand canvasbacks were being shot daily on the Chesapeake to meet the demand by tidewater epicures in the early 1870s.

From 1846 to 1847, one market hunter, according to accounts in *American Sportsman*, took more than seven thousand canvasbacks while hunting in both spring and fall. When one considers the reproductive capacity of that many birds, it's easy to see that a single such gunner, in the span of a year, could remove several thousand birds from future canvasback populations. And when you multiply the impact of this one

Though this is a picture of a hunter at the Horn Point Club near Back Bay, Virginia, taken in 1907, market gunners of the period used similar sets to take their birds. The gun being used here is probably an Auto-5 designed by John Browning. Courtesy Archie Johnson/ Gun Clubs & Decoys.

shooter by the numbers of market gunners working the tidewaters during the same period, it's easy to understand the canvasback's eventual decline.

By the mid-nineteenth century, gunning clubs began to appear up and down the Atlantic seaboard. The famed Currituck Club was likely the earliest to form, in 1857, and was soon followed by many others serving gunners who saw no limit to the supply of birds. For the twenty-two years spanning the end of the 1800s and the beginning of the 1900s, more than seventy thousand ducks, geese, and swans were taken by members of the Currituck Club alone, a testimony to the remarkable resilience of local wildfowl populations. The annual fall flight of ducks across America during that period was said to be 400 million, roughly six times the present fall flight index.

As canvasbacks and several other duck species waned, market gunners demanded more money for their take to satisfy a seemingly in-

Collector Don Farlow of Quinby, Virginia, poses with a punt gun made for market gunning in Baltimore, Maryland, by the Hall Rifle Company circa 1860. These guns exacted heavy tolls of waterfowl during both spring and fall. Courtesy Archie Johnson/ Gun Clubs & Decoys.

Canvasbacks were once prized targets of market gunners who worked ruthlessly to supply East Coast restaurants with the birds. Photo by Scott Nielsen, courtesy Ducks Unlimited, Inc.

Market gunners exacted heavy tolls on wildfowl from the fabled waters of Chesapeake Bay to California's Central Valley. Because of pleas from sportsmen, the practice was finally halted but not before waterfowl populations suffered tremendous losses from both spring and fall gunning.

satiable appetite for wildfowl among patrons of the East's finest restaurants. In 1873, an article in *Forest & Stream* listed waterfowl prices in the New York markets: swans, $2; geese, 75 cents; canvasbacks, $1 a pair; redheads, black ducks, and mallards, 75 cents a pair. The same market gunners sold duck hearts, gizzards, and livers for 25 cents a bucket on the streets of New York City.

By 1912, markets in the famed waterfowling community of Havre de Grace, Maryland, paid $3 for a pair of canvasbacks and as much as $2 for a brace of redheads. Prices for ducks in the Great Lakes region were lower—probably more a reflection of the regional economy than of the demand for wild ducks. A canvasback brought only 30 to 40 cents by the end of the nineteenth century, even though all the finest restaurants in the Twin Cities of Minnesota featured wild duck on the menu.

This collection of brant succumbed to a sole market gunner who supplied restaurants along the Atlantic tidewaters with fowl for epicureans who, by the turn of the century, had developed an insatiable appetite for wildfowl. Courtesy of the Library of Congress.

Market hunting also made its way south—albeit to a lesser extent than in the East. An 1874 edition of *Forest & Stream* recounts an effective method for taking wildfowl in Texas: "Corn was soaked in a preparation of alcohol and opium, and then scattered around the shores of the lake. . . . After devouring the corn, the geese tumble over and wallow in the mud like any other drunken goose."

Other locations that had become widely known as superb waterfowling areas—thanks to the expansion of the railroads—included California's Suisun Marsh, located on the north end of San Francisco

Bay, and Heron Lake in Minnesota. Reelfoot Lake in Tennessee inspired one turn-of-the-century scribe to write: "I am quite sure there is no place in the Union where such a body of water can be found with such remarkable natural advantages for duck shooting of every description. . . ."

After the Eastern Shore, Lake Koshkonong in eastern Wisconsin provided some of the best canvasback hunting found anywhere in America. The lake's abundant wild celery supply and a shoreline rimmed with wild rice made it particularly alluring to canvasbacks and other diving ducks. *Forest & Stream* profiled the lake in 1873 and described the best way to reach this waterfowling El Dorado: "Take the N.W. Railway . . . from Chicago to Fort Atkinson, 111 miles, thence by team three miles south."

Railroad helped expand the reach of market gunners who saw no end to America's waterfowl supplies. The 1918 Migratory Bird Treaty Act helped bring an end to unregulated gunning, giving birds unprecedented protection. Courtesy of the Library of Congress.

It is very likely that in this region, today called the Mississippi Flyway, the very first American duck calls were made. Logically, one would expect duck calls to have originated in the East, with its keen interest in waterfowling dating back to the start of the nineteenth century. Diving ducks were the primary quarry of eastern hunters, however, and these birds are not as vocal as are puddle ducks, such as mallards. Since divers do not respond readily to calling and could be easily lured within gun range merely through the use of decoys, there was no real need for easterners to develop a duck call. Along the Mississippi River, the vocal mallard comprised a major portion of the ducks taken by hunters. Those who mimicked the mallard's quack with a call substantially improved their odds compared with hunters who used only decoys.

The first game calls were probably developed in Europe in the mid-sixteenth century—gaming horns that employed metal reeds to produce sound. Adolphe Sax, the Belgian instrument maker who invented the saxophone about 1840, may have created one of the earliest duck calls. This call produced sound from a wooden reed, resembling that of a saxophone.

Noted waterfowling historian Howard Harlan, writing about a combination game call dating back to about 1640, said: "This unique 'Guckyuck' call combines calls for ducks, geese, stag, fox, roe deer, and other game." American Elam Fisher likely discovered this European call; after traveling there he brought the design back to the states, where he received a patent for a tongue-pincher call in 1870. These devices were difficult to blow effectively, leading some sporting writers to lament the use of duck calls altogether. "Artificial duck calls are contrived, as a general rule, more with a view of decoying the unwary buyer than to lead the ducks to destruction," penned one critic. "We in the East have heard more good goose callers than duck callers and our Eastern gunners mostly use their own throats." It is also likely that the Cree and other Indians used their own voices to call ducks and geese long before Europeans ever set foot on North America.

"After a few blows," wrote Nash Buckingham in an article referring to the quality of early calls, "their reeds either jammed, rattled

The Broadbill Duck Call

A Call that Calls

The true to life tone, is your best substitute for live decoys.

Ask your Dealer, or $1.00 Postpaid.

N. C. Hansen Co., Zimmerman, Minn.

This advertisement from the October 1939 issue of Sports Afield *is peddling the early Broadbill Duck Call. Note the ad suggests that this is ". . . your best substitute for live decoys."*

helplessly and dejectedly out of tune, or else bit one's tongue." It wasn't until call-maker Perry Hooker taught Buckingham how to use a duck call that he gained confidence in them and eventually fashioned calls of his own. By 1900 there were call makers up and down the flyway, and technological advances were improving tone quality. The area surrounding the Illinois River and the country adjacent to Reelfoot Lake in Tennessee are the two cradles of American duck calls.

Philip Sanford Olt, founder of the venerable P. S. Olt call company, grew up in Pekin, Illinois, and frequently hunted in the vicinity of the Illinois River. He made several innovations in duck calls, including many improvements on the early metal reed calls. Olt's famous D-2 call set the standard for duck calls of the period, indelibly stamping his name in the memory of waterfowlers for generations to come. "Olt must be given credit for the groove and cork design," wrote Harlan in his book, *Duck Calls*, "and as its inventor he produced calls that are considered to be the forerunners of the modern-day Arkansas-style call." Sales of Olt and other duck calls quadrupled in a relatively short span after the use of live decoys was outlawed in 1935.

John Moses Browning was one of the world's great gun pioneers, introducing innovative designs that are still in use today. He's pictured here with his famous A-5 repeater, a gun that won quick favor among waterfowlers. Courtesy Browning Arms Company.

The technology of waterfowling guns was advancing rapidly as well. The large punt-mounted guns of the eastern tidewater regions were gradually replaced by smaller repeating shotguns. Gun-design pioneer John Browning invented the first repeating shotgun—a lever action, five-shot 12 gauge—in 1886. It quickly became a favorite of market gunners, who continued to take awesome numbers of birds. Winchester's model 1897, a five-shot pump, was another favorite among turn-of-the-century waterfowlers. Browning's invention of

THE PARKER GUN

BEST AND LOWEST PRICÉ GUN IN THE WORLD.

HAMMERLESS AND ✳

✳ HAMMER GUNS

SOLD BY THE TRADE EVERYWHERE.

Descriptive Catalogue Mailed on Application.

MANUFACTURED BY

PARKER BROS.,

Meriden, Conn.

Show Rooms 97 Chambers St., New York.

Illustration from Shooting on Upland, Marsh, and Stream, *1890.*

Here's a selection of classic old cartridges from the Howard Harlan collection. Note the all-metal case at left. Photo by Chris Dorsey.

the autoloading shotgun in 1905, however, redefined the notion of the perfect waterfowling gun across the country.

Duck populations could not keep up with the unregulated assault by growing numbers of increasingly better-equipped waterfowlers. Grinnell openly complained of decreases in ducks and geese in 1901, calling for a nationwide ban on spring waterfowl shooting. The logs of famous waterfowling clubs across the country told the story: In 1882, members of the Winous Point club, near Port Clinton, Ohio, took a record 1,987 redheads, and in 1900—a mere eight years later—only one redhead was shot. Similar declines took place in canvasback harvests: more than 660 were taken at Winous Point in 1880; only one was felled during the autumn of 1900.

By 1883, many sportsmen's groups and periodicals called for a ban on the use of the devastating punt guns. The same sportsmen also wanted an end to using these guns for nighttime shooting of waterfowl. Market gunning on Chesapeake Bay was outlawed altogether in 1918, ending the uncontrolled assault on wildfowl populations in the region. Spring shooting was banned nationwide the same year, an overdue acknowledgment of the excesses of the previous half century.

This turn-of-the-century photo depicts the practice of shooting from a sink box near Havre de Grace, Maryland. The technique was commonly used for hunting brant and both diving and sea ducks. Photo from the Don Cole, Jr., collection, courtesy of the Havre de Grace Decoy Museum..

As taxing as the over-gunning was on North America's waterfowl populations, it was ultimately a combination of the drought and the Great Depression that brought an end to the "glory" years of waterfowling. Many out-of-work Americans turned to the country's game supply to feed their families, increasing poaching to unprecedented levels. Law enforcement was ill-equipped to cope with the onslaught, and the diaries left by wardens of the period indicate an understandable reluctance to arrest poachers whose children might otherwise have gone hungry.

The fabric of present-day American waterfowling is woven from what is arguably the most storied and long-lived sporting tradition found in the New World. At the center of our waterfowling heritage

WILL YOU HELP?

FIRE LIGHTERS
The Arch Enemies of All True Sportsmen

Will You Help to Bring Such Men to Justice?

Since the days of the first market hunter, men have shot wild fowl at night by the aid of artificial light. Whether this was done by the light of a driftwood fire on a point where the birds were passing over, or by a kerosene torch from a boat, in which was strapped a huge swivel gun, the process was called fire lighting.

Modern inventions have given the fire lighter the acetylene and electric spot-lights. In many sections unscrupulous pot-hunters still bewilder huge flocks of birds at night, cutting paths of destruction through the huddled masses of roosting birds, not for sport but for meat and personal gain.

The Public Shooting Ground—Game Refuge Bill, S. 1452 in the United States Senate and H. R. 5823 in the House of Representatives, will not only provide sanctuaries where migratory birds may nest, rest and feed unmolested by man, but it will provide a warden force sufficient to bring these violators of the law into camp where they will receive their just deserts.

It is hoped that this bill will be enacted into law at the present session of Congress. The time is urgent now for you to write your Senators and Representatives, requesting that they support it.

Do not forget that the American Game Protective Association is your national organization, fighting your battles for "More Game" and better sport.

Join the Association and do your part. Fill out the coupon and mail it today.

This advertisement appeared in the January 1923 issue of Outdoor Life. *Waterfowlers of the period urged an end to the practice of fire lighting in which large numbers of the birds were shot at night.*

are the birds that have drawn generations of wildfowlers to the sloughs and marshes. If the history of wildfowling has taught us anything, it's that the future of the sport depends on the decisions of the past and present.

An American Waterfowling Timeline

A.D. 800—First-known decoy (canvasback) is fashioned by Native Americans from feathers and rushes. The decoy is discovered in Lovelock Cave, Nevada, in 1924.

Early 1700s—Massachusetts Colony passes first waterfowl hunting law, banning the use of camouflaged canoes and sailboats when hunting ducks and geese.

1811—Massive earthquake strikes New Madrid, Missouri. Mississippi River is reported to flow north for several minutes and Reelfoot Lake is formed in Tennessee, later to become one of the best-known waterfowling areas on the Mississippi Flyway.

1831—The shotgun game of trap is introduced from England.

1838—New York legislature bans the use of sink boxes.

1849—Congress passes the Swamp Land Act, beginning the systematic and subsidized destruction of American wetlands.

1855—Birth of John Moses Browning, perhaps the most innovative gun designer in American history.

1864—George Perkins Marsh pens *Man and Nature*, ushering in the American conservation movement.

1866—Glass balls replace live pigeons as the standard target in shotgunning games.

1870—Philip Sanford Olt is born near Pekin, Illinois. He later founded the famed P. S. Olt call company and is credited as the inventor of the Arkansas-style duck call.

1870s—Sportsmen begin working in earnest to pass restrictions on commercial hunting and fishing. Hats stuffed with feathers become the fashion rage. *Forest & Stream* and *American Field* editors call for a ban on spring shooting of wildfowl.

1871—First game preserve was formed in Pike County, Pennsylvania. *American Sportsman*, a monthly tabloid, begins publishing in October and, as one historian noted, its launch "marked a watershed in environmental history." Through the pages of *American Sportsman*, sportsmen/conservationists plead for an end to commercialization of wildlife.

1872—Maryland becomes the first state to provide "rest days" for ducks and geese. Yellowstone Park is created.

1873—Remington introduces its first double-barreled shotgun. Previously, double guns were imported from Europe and were too expensive for average waterfowlers.

1874—*Forest & Stream*, forerunner of *Field & Stream*, begins publishing and adds to the chorus of voices from American sportsmen calling for expanded conservation efforts.

1875—Commercial hunting of waterfowl is outlawed in Arkansas.

1876—Influential cartoonist and waterfowl conservationist Jay Norwood "Ding" Darling is born in Norwood, Michigan.

1878—Labrador duck becomes extinct.

1879—Illinois Farm Drainage Act is passed, accelerating the rate at which that state's wetlands are drained. This act began the destruction of Illinois' wetlands; now less than 15 percent remain. George Ligowski invents the first clay pigeon, the forerunner of the modern clay target.

1880—With the aid of his brothers, John Browning establishes his arms factory.

1881—George Bird Grinnell formulates theory of democratic game protection.

1883—American Ornithologists Union is formed, consisting mostly of devout bird hunters.

1886—Audubon Society is founded by sportsman-naturalist George Bird Grinnell. Patent No. 336,287 is granted for the Winchester Model 1887, a lever-action repeating shotgun.

1887—Theodore Roosevelt helps launch the Boone and Crockett Club.

1892—President Benjamin Harrison creates the first combination National Wildlife Refuge and Wilderness Area.

1893—First Grand American Handicap Trap Shoot is held at Dexter Park, New York.

1894—*Forest & Stream* calls for an end to the commercialization of game.

1900—Lacey Act is passed, outlawing market hunting and the interstate shipment of wildlife.

1901—Theodore Roosevelt is elected president and launches sweeping conservation initiatives. George Bird Grinnell writes *American Duck Shooting*, the first book devoted solely to American waterfowling.

1902—Gun-design genius John Browning introduces first autoloading shotgun.

1912—Dwight W. Huntington founds Game Conservation Society in New York.

1913—Weeks-McLean bill becomes law, giving responsibility for managing migratory game birds to the U.S. Bureau of Biological Survey.

1914—Last passenger pigeon dies in the Cincinnati Zoo, a poignant reminder of the perils of habitat destruction and unregulated shooting.

1916—Convention is signed between the United States and England (on behalf of Canada) to protect migratory game birds passing between the two countries.

1918—Federal Migratory Bird Treaty Act is passed, prohibiting spring shooting and establishing a daily bag limit of twenty-five ducks.

1923—The first-ever decoy exhibition is held in Bellport, Long Island.

1924—James E. Burns invents the first noncorrosive primer for Remington, a major advancement that eliminated the need to clean gun bores after each firing.

1926—John Browning dies in Liege, Belgium.

1929—Norbeck-Andersen Migratory Bird Conservation Act provides funds to purchase additional waterfowl refuge lands.

1930s—Severe drought strikes plains states and gives rise to the Dust Bowl of the "Dirty Thirties."

1930—Formation of More Game Birds Foundation, forerunner of Ducks Unlimited.

1931—American Wild Fowlers consolidates with More Game Birds Foundation. Labrador Retriever Club holds first American retriever field trial on December 21.

1934—President Franklin Roosevelt appoints special presidential committee to develop recommendations to restore migratory waterfowl. Ding Darling, Aldo Leopold, and Tom Beck, president of More Game Birds Foundation (forerunner to Ducks Unlimited), serve as the committee. Duck stamp concept is approved by Congress, thanks to the efforts of Ding Darling. The first national all-breed retriever field trial is held, with fifteen entries.

1935—Live decoys are outlawed nationally and the first International Wild Duck Census is undertaken—considered the grandfather of waterfowl surveys.

1936—First North American Wildlife Conference is held. Thomas E. Walsh, of Greenville, Mississippi, wins the first-ever World Championship Duck Calling Contest, in Stuttgart, Arkansas.

1937—Pittman-Robertson Federal Aid in Wildlife Restoration is passed by the urging of sportsmen, establishing an excise tax on sporting-equipment sales. The money is earmarked for wildlife conservation programs. Ducks Unlimited is incorporated in Washington, D.C. The U.S. Senate ratifies a treaty with Mexico to protect migratory birds and mammals passing between the two countries.

1938—Ducks Unlimited Canada is formed and begins work on its first project at Big Grass Marsh, Manitoba.

1940—Bureau of Biological Survey merges with Bureau of Fisheries to form U.S. Fish & Wildlife Service. USDA's Agricultural Conservation Program is launched, leading to the eventual draining of more than 57 million acres of wetlands.

1944—More ducks reported on North American prairies than in previous thirty years.

1948—Patsy Fricke wins the first-ever Women's World Championship Duck Calling Contest held in Stuttgart, Arkansas.

1949—J. E. "Jake" Gartner becomes the first person to win three consecutive World Championship Duck Calling contests held in Stuttgart, Arkansas.

1956—J. C. Higgins begins selling the first commercial gas-operated autoloader, the Model 60.

1971—Ramsar Treaty is signed, providing framework for international protection of wetlands important to migratory birds.

1973—Browning introduces highly successful 12 gauge Citori over/under.

1974—Ducks Unlimited Mexico and Ducks Unlimited New Zealand are formed.

1976—Gore-Tex is introduced, the first successful waterproof and breathable fabric; it redefines comfort in sporting garments.

1977—President Jimmy Carter signs Executive Order 11990, which establishes wetland protection as an official policy of the federal government.

1985—Congress passes the "swampbuster" provision of the Food Security Act, denying federal subsidies to any farmer who knowingly converts wetlands to farmland.

1988—Remington sells its three millionth Model 1100 autoloading shotgun.

1992—Ducks Unlimited membership stands at 578,531, and $58.7 million is raised, with nearly 7 million acres conserved throughout the organization's history.

1993—A checkered duck call made by early call-maker Victor Glado brings $16,500 at a Ward Foundation auction in Salisbury, Maryland, the most ever paid for a duck call.

II

*W*aterfowlers of Note

There have been many forks in the long road leading to the current state of our wildfowl. All too often, the quest for short-term profits led to the path of wetland destruction, sacrificing the very health of the land upon which we depend. One can only imagine the state of our wetlands and waterfowl had it not been for the work of a handful of dedicated early American conservationists who had the vision to recognize the trends of habitat destruction. They knew what had to be done, and they had the vigilance to make vital changes. Some tackled issues directly; others used the written word or personal influence to guide the course of American conservation. Virtually all of these men stood against the conventional wisdom of their day—often alienating friends, readers, and constituents—looking past the gains of the moment for the benefit of future wildlife populations. They were, in a word, leaders.

The next time you watch a flight of wood ducks weave through a stand of flooded timber, marvel at a flock of mallards as they parachute toward your decoys, or are mesmerized by thousands of migrating pintail, remember the fragile nature of their existence. Never forget the men who stood before you—people who once shared your reverence for the same wild wings of autumn—for to them all waterfowlers owe a great debt. With that debt comes responsibility, a duty we carry with us to ensure that future generations will know the

Theodore Roosevelt (left). Courtesy Wildlife Management Institute.

majesty of wildfowling and all that goes with it. Here, then, are the people who made a difference.

George Bird Grinnell (1849–1938) was instrumental in forming the Boone and Crockett Club, the first American conservation organization. As the editor of *Forest & Stream*, Grinnell worked diligently to advance sporting ethics, penning numerous stories on that theme. He was greatly influenced by John James Audubon's widow, who served as his early teacher, instilling in him a keen interest in natural history. In 1866, in honor of Audubon, Grinnell formed the Audubon Society of New York—forerunner of the National Audubon Society. He began a friendship with Theodore Roosevelt and helped develop the American national park and forest system. He also served on the first advisory

George Bird Grinnell. Courtesy National Audubon Society.

board for Federal Migratory Bird Law and in 1901 wrote the first American book on waterfowling, *American Duck Shooting*.

Jay Norwood "Ding" Darling (1876–1962) was a satirical cartoonist for the *Des Moines Register*, winning the Pulitzer Prize for his work in both 1923 and 1942. His poignant cartoons drew accolades from around the country and helped bring the desperate plight of waterfowl

Ding Darling. Courtesy Ding Darling Foundation.

This is the inaugural duck stamp penned in 1935 by conservation pioneer and Pulitzer Prize winning cartoonist Ding Darling. Courtesy Ducks Unlimited Archives.

to the attention of Washington politicians. David Lendt, in his biography of Darling, wrote that "he was so famous the *New York Globe* facetiously suggested that 'the Centennial at Philadelphia was laid down in the year 1876 in order to coincide with the birth of Ding Darling.'" Like so many of America's foremost conservation leaders, Darling was a waterfowler who knew a hunter must also be a conservationist. His affinity for wildfowl was clear throughout his fifty-year career, as his cartoons regularly featured the problems facing waterfowl across America. He was also a key figure in developing the federal duck stamp and drew the inaugural print. That program has since generated nearly $500 million for waterfowl conservation. In 1934, President Franklin Roosevelt appointed Darling to a panel to recommend a course of action that would restore the nation's migratory waterfowl.

'BYE NOW_IT'S BEEN WONDERFUL KNOWING YOU.

Ding's Farewell

The Des Moines Register—Tuesday, Feb. 13, 1962

This was Ding Darling's last cartoon. The outspoken conservation proponent entrusted this illustration to his secretary to be used after his death. It appeared the morning after he died in 1962. The nation lost one of its great environmental leaders, but by teaching a generation of Americans that they could make a difference, his legacy lives on. Courtesy of the Ding Darling Foundation.

Aldo Leopold. Photo by Robert McCabe, courtesy University of Wisconsin Archives.

Aldo Leopold (1886–1948), the father of American conservation, wrote the now-immortal *A Sand County Almanac,* a work for which he posthumously received the John Burroughs Medal in 1978. He served with the U.S. Forest Service before being appointed to chair the newly created Game Management Department at the University of Wisconsin. He wrote his pioneering book *Game Management,* in 1933. Leopold worked extensively with Ding Darling to improve the condition of the continental waterfowl population. He also served as director of the National Audubon Society and helped found the Wilderness Society in 1935. His concept of a land ethic is still widely studied by conservation students across the continent. Leopold died shortly after being named an adviser on conservation to the United Nations.

Nash Buckingham (1880–1971) worked a pen with the same artistry that his many friends saw him use when swinging his famous Bo-Whoop shotgun on passing mallards. Though best known for his en-

Nash Buckingham. Photo by Charles W. Schwartz, courtesy Chubby Andrews.

tertaining style of writing about waterfowling, he was one of the first
of his day to speak against the excesses of overharvesting wildfowl—
long before doing so was in vogue. He also served four years as executive secretary of a national group called Wild Fowlers, a Washington,
D.C.–based organization dedicated to restoring duck and goose populations.

Van Campen Heilner (1899–1970) wrote *A Book on Duck Shooting*, regarded by many as one of the most vivid accounts of the waterfowler's life ever written. His articles appeared frequently in *National Sportsman*, *Sports Afield*, and *Field & Stream*. In 1918, Heilner became associate editor of *Field & Stream*, a post he often used to advance the cause of waterfowl conservation. In addition, he was an authentic American character whose diverse life included expeditions to Cuba, Alaska, and Peru, bit roles in Will Rogers' movies, and flying a plane over Pikes Peak. Heilner hunted waterfowl across North America and in scores of foreign countries, shooting with many notables of the day.

Ira Gabrielson (1889–1977) oversaw the formation of the U.S. Fish and Wildlife Service, serving as its first director in 1940. Aside from

Ira Gabrielson seated at right. Courtesy of the Wildlife Management Institute.

being an avid waterfowler, he presided over the Wildlife Management Institute and helped found not only the International Union for the Conservation of Nature and Natural Resources, but also the World Wildlife Fund. He wrote *Wildlife Conservation* in 1941 and *Wildlife Refuges* in 1943. Gabrielson was awarded the Distinguished Service Medal from the U.S. Department of the Interior in 1948.

Gordon MacQuarrie (1900–1956) graduated from the University of Wisconsin in 1923. He eventually became the outdoor editor of the *Milwaukee Journal* and wrote for most of the major sporting periodicals of his day. He gained a widespread following for his fictitious Old Duck Hunters' Association, the vehicle he used to entertain and enlighten the many thousands of waterfowlers across the country who counted themselves among his fans. "He was a pioneer, and a dedicated conservationist," wrote Zack Taylor, "when it was neither fash-

Gordon MacQuarrie. Courtesy The Milwaukee Journal.

ionable nor polite to be one." The Wisconsin Academy of Sciences, Arts, and Letters semiannually presents an award in MacQuarrie's honor for excellence in conservation communication.

Jimmy Robinson (1897–1986) was a well-known *Sports Afield* writer whose passion for waterfowl hunting is evident in the pages of his large body of work. His yearly duck survey was a staple for waterfowlers of the day. He received numerous conservation awards and was one of the earliest writers to introduce an upstart conservation organization called Ducks Unlimited to a national sporting audience. Robinson later served as a trustee emeritus of Ducks Unlimited.

Jimmy Robinson. Courtesy Sports Afield.

III

Gunning for Success

When a crude form of gunpowder—a mixture of saltpeter (potassium nitrate), sulfur, and charcoal—passed from Asia to Europe in the thirteenth century, the world was forever changed. As the stone fortresses of oppressive nobility crumbled under cannon fire, the entire European social order underwent a metamorphosis as the gap between royalty and common man narrowed.

In the early 1600s, the first crude shotguns appeared, offering many advantages over the muskets of the day—not least of which was the ability to shoot birds in flight. With the advent of the scattergun came the birth of wingshooting.

Early shotguns had limited effective ranges, for barrel choking wasn't introduced until after the American Civil War. Unchoked guns did well to place more than 40 percent of their shot in a 30-inch circle at 40 yards. Gun historians still debate the origins of the revolutionary concept of choking. With little conclusive evidence to determine whether American Fred Kimble or Englishman W. R. Pape was first to develop the shotgun choke, any statement favoring one over the other probably has more to do with which side of the Atlantic one lives on than with fact.

The invention of the first practical, all-brass, center-fire shotgun shells helped usher in the breech-loading shotgun by the mid-1800s. By the 1870s, a less-expensive shell, consisting of a brass head and a

Illustration from American Duck, Goose & Brant Shooting, *1929.*

tightly wound paper body, was introduced. Unlike the all-brass shells, the paper cartridges were sold already loaded from the factory, another notable step in the evolution of shotgunning.

GUNS AND THEIR MAKE

Prior to 1873, most double-barreled guns were the product of British gunsmiths, works of art out of reach of the average American fowler. But in 1873, Remington introduced its first double-barreled shotgun— armament in keeping with Remington's established tradition of producing quality guns with affordable price tags. As fine as it was, the Remington offering didn't supplant the well-established British dou-

Illustration from Shooting on Upland, Marsh, and Stream, *1890.*

bles. In fact, it wasn't until A. H. Fox began producing fine double guns in 1906 that European gunmakers began to think of America as something other than a nation of rifle makers and shooters. Pragmatic Americans, however, found pump guns more to their liking. Hammer trombone, or pump guns, appeared about the mid-1880s. A significant advancement in pump guns occurred in 1904, when Stevens introduced the Model 520, the first hammerless pump gun.

Perhaps no pump gun ever reached the notoriety of Winchester's famed Model 12, released in 1912. The Model 12 became the standard by which all other pumps would be judged. Its quality machining and smooth operation have never been matched, nor are they likely to be, for producing such quality today would price the gun beyond the range of its intended market.

Many waterfowlers have grown fond of repeaters like the Beretta A303 (above) and the venerable Browning A-5. Auto-loaders eliminate the need to cycle rounds by working a pump, and offer an extra shot that their double gun counterparts do not. Photo by Chris Dorsey.

On December 17, 1901, a bellwether date in the history of shotgunning, legendary gun designer John Browning received a patent for his now-famous Auto-5 repeating shotgun. The A-5's effectiveness soon won it an ardent following among hunters and market gunners, who admired its efficiency. While the Brits looked upon the American autoloaders as the creations of Philistines, shooters who employed them grew fond of the guns' ability to cycle rounds without needing a pump. Technological advances helped win more fans of the autoloaders, improving their reliability and convincing a generation of shooters that autoloaders were the guns of the future. Despite the Brits' overall distaste for the American guns, there was no denying their efficiency. In *Shotgunning Trends in Transition*, author Don Zutz asks a poignant question: ". . . if classic side-by-sides are such effective guns, why aren't they in greater demand among serious skeet, trap, and sporting clays competitors?"

This is not to say that early autoloaders had no drawbacks. Most early entries could not readily cycle different loads without mechani-

Four of today's favorite 12-gauge waterfowling autoloaders. Top to bottom: the Browning A-5, Remington Model 11-87 with synthetic stock, Beretta A390ST, and Benelli Super Black Eagle with 3½-inch chamber. Each has proven its worth in duck blinds across the world.

cal adjustments. Surprisingly enough, the first 12 gauge autoloader that could handle most 12 gauge loads without jamming was introduced by Smith & Wesson, the now-famous handgun maker.

Another breakthrough in "shotgunningdom" occurred when James Burns invented the first noncorrosive primer for Remington in 1924. This development meant that hunters no longer had to laboriously clean their barrels after only a few firings. Two years later, following further refinement, new noncorrosive cartridges were ready for mass-market release.

In 1960, the first plastic shotshell hulls were introduced, ushering in the modern era of shotshell reloading. Mayville Engineering Company (MEC), the venerable Wisconsin company that manufactures shotshell reloaders, has sold more than 2.5 million reloaders, testament to the popularity of reusable shotshells. The plastic hulls decay at a geologic pace, however, and hunters who leave their hulls behind in the field contribute to an insidious form of pollution. In Zutz's words, ". . .there is little difference between pitching a beer can from a car window and dropping empty plastic hulls into the marsh."

LEAD, STEEL, AND IGNORANCE

Listen to conversations around modern duck clubs, and you're apt to believe that hunters never missed when using lead shot. Conversely, steel shot, some contend, is to blame for everything from high crippling rates on ducks to high blood pressure in hunters. Like it or not, the evidence that lead shot was poisoning millions of waterfowl and other species led to the initial steps that banned lead shot for waterfowl hunting. Despite what is commonly believed, the U.S. Fish & Wildlife Service never intended lead shot to be banned for waterfowl hunting nationwide. Instead, wrote biologist William Anderson in a report for the International Waterfowl and Wetlands Research Bureau (IWWRB), "in a twist of irony, legal actions intended to restrict the use of nontoxic shot ultimately had the opposite effect. The federal government's original plan in 1976 called for converting only those counties in which an average of greater than two waterfowl per square mile

American Hunter *editor Tom Fulgham scans the skies for more snow geese during a field test of new Winchester steel shot loads.* Photo by Chris Dorsey.

were harvested annually. Thanks to legal actions, this plan was never fully implemented, and the ensuing legal tug-of-war eventually manifested in the court-reinforced decision to require nontoxic shot for all waterfowl hunting throughout the United States."

Though it may make little sense to require steel shot for, say, goose hunting in a field where it is perfectly legal to hunt pheasants or other upland game with lead shot, there is a widespread consensus among wildlife biologists that lead shot poses a hazard to waterfowl in areas where gunners repeatedly use it. One prominent researcher who agrees with this position is Dr. Glen Sanderson, of the Illinois Natural History Survey, the dean of American waterfowl biologists. In his 1992 report for the IWWRB, he stated: "I believe that lead poisoning in wild waterfowl is a serious problem in most places where waterfowl are hunted with lead shot. We know that lead is toxic to most, if not all, living organisms. I believe that it is time to stop adding lead shot to wetlands and upland areas heavily used by waterfowl and other game birds that are prone to ingest lead pellets." In one U.S. Fish & Wildlife Service study, it was estimated that roughly 6.5 million birds were saved thanks to the switch from lead to steel shot in heavily hunted areas from 1986 to 1991.

Still, many hunters are skeptical and contend that steel shot has substantially increased the number of crippled ducks. The loss of more wounded birds, the argument goes, offsets the number of birds saved by the switch from lead to steel. When scientifically tested, however, steel shot performed as well as lead in bringing birds to hand. Could it be that poor shooters found a handy alibi for their inability to kill birds when steel shot came on the waterfowling scene?

The search for a nontoxic alternative to steel continued, however, with nearly forty attempts being made—and failing. In some cases, the new shot was too expensive to produce in quantity. In other instances, the chosen substances held no ballistical advantage over steel. Others were lead-based and, therefore, ultimately doomed to fail the tough toxicity standards set by the U.S. Fish & Wildlife Service. One such shot was developed by Canadian John Brown, a carpenter by trade and a waterfowler by passion. His nickel-plated lead shot held the ballistic requirements of an effective waterfowl load, but failed to pass as a nontoxic alternative to steel shot.

Brown's search continued, however. He discovered that a substance called bismuth—the active ingredient in the widely used digestive medicine Pepto Bismol—had many of the handling properties of lead, with a specific gravity roughly halfway between that of iron (steel) and lead. Bismuth's density advantage allows it to retain energy longer and, because you don't have to compensate with larger, less-dense shot—as is the case with steel—you can expect better pattern density.

Buoyed by his initial tests of homemade bismuth shot, Brown took his idea to Los Angeles publisher Robert E. Petersen, a well-known shooter and collector of fine double shotguns. Petersen had long been interested in finding a nontoxic alternative to steel, preferably a new shot that wouldn't damage the thinly walled barrels of his high-dollar guns. Thanks to Petersen's financial backing of extensive toxicity studies, the U.S. Fish & Wildlife Service appeared ready to approve bismuth as a nontoxic substance for shot, giving American waterfowlers a choice of shots for the first time since the nationwide ban on lead for waterfowling was implemented in 1991. Questions about the world supply of bismuth and the cost of producing bismuth cartridges remain, so it is still unclear how the market will respond to this shot—especially as the many steel shot detractors come to discover that they are as apt to miss with bismuth as they were with steel and lead.

Screw-in choke systems have added a great deal of versatility to modern fowling pieces; changing a gun's choke is now as simple as changing the tubes. Courtesy Beretta U.S.A.

<u>USING STEEL</u>

Some of the criticism against steel is not without merit. Early steel loads suffered from a technological time lag, since steel shot posed new problems for gun and ammunition manufacturers. Slow-burning powders had to be used to keep the hard steel pellets from binding in the chamber and cone bore portions of a shotgun. Unlike lead, the steel pellets would not readily deform to accommodate the payload passing through the constricted choke. Under too much pressure and too tight a choke, steel shot posed the risk of causing ring bulging in a gun's bore.

Early steel loads also lacked the wet-proofing of modern loads; if they got wet—an inherent likelihood when waterfowling—the shot would rust. While such pellets would not form a solid steel slug as is often thought, rusted pellets could lose some of their aerodynamic properties. Most steel shot used today is coated with a microlayer of copper or other rust inhibitor. High-density plastic shotcups also had to be developed to protect barrels from the hardened shot.

None of this changed the fact that the lighter steel pellets lose their energy faster than do lead pellets. Despite what some hunters believe, steel shot is not larger than lead shot. Shot sizes are identical; that is, a No. 4 steel pellet and a No. 4 lead pellet are both .130 inch in diameter. The difference, then, is that steel pellets weigh about 30 percent less than do lead pellets of the same size. This is behind the concept of selecting steel pellets two or three shot sizes larger than the lead shot used for waterfowling.

The idea is straightforward enough. If you use No. 4 lead, for instance, you'll want to switch to No. 2 steel to approximate the ballistic property of the lead 4s. The larger steel pellets will retain their energy longer, compensating for steel's inherent shortcoming in density. It's true that with larger shot there will be fewer pellets per shell, but the perfectly round steel pellets help offset this loss by distributing a more even pattern than does lead shot, which is often swaged in the firing process.

Understanding Dram Equivalents

Dram equivalent is an archaic term that equates the velocity of today's smokeless powders with the black powder of yesteryear. A shotshell with a 3½-dram equivalent for example, is equal in velocity to 3½ drams of old-fashioned black powder. Dram equivalents, then, are a measure of powder to velocity.

Pattern/Pellet Density & Energy Guide

Look up distance to your game for recommended pellet. Pellets appropriate for longer distances may also be used at shorter range. Use of pellets at distances surpassing their listing is not recommended.

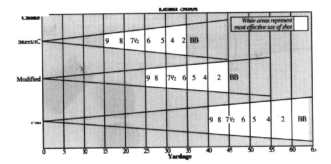

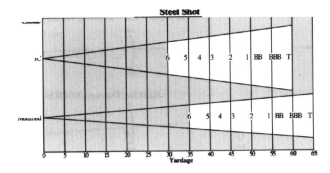

Courtesy Winchester Arms.

Standard Shot Sizes

Buckshot Sizes			Shot Sizes			
Shot Number	Diameter in Inches	# Pellets Typical Loads	Shot Number	Diameter in Inches	Pellets/oz. Lead	Pellets/oz. Steel
#4	.24	27 34 41	9	.08	585	–
			8	.09	410	–
#3	.25	20 24	7½	.095	350	–
			6	.11	225	316
#1	.30	12 16 20 24	5	.12	170	243
			4	.13	135	191
0	.32	12	3	.14	–	153
			2	.15	87	125
00	.33	9 12 15 18	1	.16	–	103
			BB	.18	50	72
000	.36	8 10	BBB	.19	–	61
			T	.20	–	53

LEAD VS. STEEL
COMPARISON CHART*

Shot Type	Wt.	Shot Size	No. Pellets	Muzzle Velocity (FPS)	Retained Energy Per Pellet (Ft. Lbs.)	
					40 Yds.	60 Yds.
Lead	1¼	6	281	1330	2.3	1.3
Steel	1¼	4	215	1365	2.5	1.4
Lead	1¼	4	169	1330	4.4	2.7
Steel	1¼	2	141	1365	4.4	2.6
Lead	1½	4	202	1260	4.1	2.6
Steel	1¼	2	156	1275	4.1	2.4
Lead	1½	2	130	1260	7.0	4.6
Steel	1¼	BB	90	1275	8.3	5.2

*Source: SAAMI Exterior Ballistics Tables Adopted 4/23/81
NOTE: Steel shot pellets two sizes larger than lead deliver comparable down range energy.

MEDIUM GEESE (LONG RANGE: BEYOND 50 YDS.)

STEEL LOAD	STEEL SHOT SIZE	SUGGESTED CHOKE
12 ga., 2¾", 1-¼ oz.	BB, BBB	IMP. MOD.
12. ga., 3", 1-¼ oz.	BB, BBB	IMP. MOD.
12 ga., 3", 1-⅜ oz.	BB, BBB	IMP. MOD., FULL
12. ga., 3½", 1-9/16 oz.	BB, BBB	IMP. MOD., FULL
10 ga., 3½", 1-¾ oz.	BB, BBB	IMP. MOD., FULL

LARGE GEESE (LONG RANGE: BEYOND 50 YDS.)

STEEL LOAD	STEEL SHOT SIZE	SUGGESTED CHOKE
12 ga., 2¾", 1-⅛ oz.	BBB, T	MOD., IMP. MOD.
12. ga., 3", 1-¼ oz.	BBB, T, TT	MOD., IMP. MOD.
12 ga., 3", 1-⅜ oz.	BBB, T, TT	MOD., IMP. MOD.
12. ga., 3½", 1-9/16 oz.	BBB, T, TT	MOD., IMP. MOD.
10 ga., 3½", 1-¾ oz.	BBB, T, TT	MOD., IMP. MOD.

Courtesy Remington Arms.

Because the harder steel shot does not deform like lead, large steel pellets can bunch up when fired through tightly choked guns. This increases stress on shotgun barrels, which can ruin patterns, cause ring bulging, and present a safety hazard to shooters. Consequently, some shotgun manufacturers recommend not shooting steel shot larger than No. 1 in guns with full choke, especially older guns that lack the stronger barrels made for shooting modern steel loads.

Selecting the best steel loads for your favorite kind of waterfowling should start at the pattern board, for each gun and load combination may bring unique results—even if both gun and shotshell are from the same factory. Having tried a number of load and choke combinations in 12 gauge, I've found that steel No. 2s perform best out of the modified 12 gauge I typically employ when duck hunting. Ballistically, that makes sense, given that the pellet energy of a No. 2 steel shot pellet is similar to a No. 4 lead pellet at 40 yards. Much has been made of the supposed tight patterning of steel shot, but experts such as Zutz and others have cautioned against assuming that steel loads will always pattern tighter than equivalent lead loads fired from the same gun. Again, test loads for yourself.

Sounds of Silence

A duck-hunting guide once told me that he could tell how much waterfowling experience a client had by how well he could hear. Sadly, that is too often the case. While the years of watching a sunrise over a marsh and the camaraderie we shared with friends bring us treasures of memories, they also bring hearing hazards. Protecting your hearing is especially important: Once the sensitive nerves of the ears have been damaged, they cannot be repaired.

A typical 12 gauge

(cont'd. next page)

I've found steel shot sizes smaller than No. 3 to be too light for most mid- to large-sized ducks, though teal readily succumb to these loads at close to medium ranges (25 to 40 yards). After comparing the relative effectiveness between the 3½-inch 12 gauge and the 10 gauge for geese, I've opted for the larger payload of the 10 gauge loaded in BBBs or Ts. The large steel pellets mean that pattern density will decrease, but the larger 10 gauge loads help offset this by providing slightly more shot capacity. The larger pellets, too, retain energy longer and can, if used by skilled wingshooters, consistently kill birds at ranges of 60 to 70 yards.

Much hyperbole has been both spoken and written about how hunters must adjust their leads when shooting steel shot. Malarkey. Lead and steel shot share similar muzzle velocities, which means the distance one leads a bird in flight with either shot should be the same. For instance, the difference in muzzle velocity between a 1⅛-ounce load of No. 2 steel and a 1¼-ounce load of No. 4 lead is only 35 feet per second—the steel being slightly faster. Translated, that means there is only two-thousandths of a second, or 1.4 inches, in lead differential at 40 yards between the two. If you're missing with steel, you will very likely miss with lead.

No matter your gun and load combination, carefully sift through recommendations from armchair waterfowling experts; otherwise, you'll be up to your gizzard in half-baked wisdom if you're not discriminating. Perhaps the best advice is to adopt a test-it-yourself approach to unsolicited advice, for it's always wise to leave the guesswork and theories to neophytes.

shotgun blast measures about 155 decibels; it takes only 140 decibels to permanently damage your hearing. The sudden shock can damage the ears' sensitive nerve cells, which turn sound vibrations into the electrical impulses that are sent to the auditory cortex, the portion of the brain where hearing is perceived.

Prolonged exposure to shotgun blasts will almost certainly take its toll on a person's hearing, though each person's ears are susceptible to varying degrees. With shorter-barreled shotguns and recoil-reducing porting systems growing in favor, hunters near such guns stand an increased risk of hearing loss. Waterfowlers are especially susceptible to hearing damage, because they are often in close proximity to other hunters—as when in a blind.

Since hearing what is happening around us is such an important part of life, selecting quality earwear should command as much attention as choosing a shotgun. Have your local hearing specialist test you for hearing loss and ask for advice on how to prevent further damage to your ears. Don't wait.

IV

Ducks and Geese of North America
Identification information and corresponding photo section

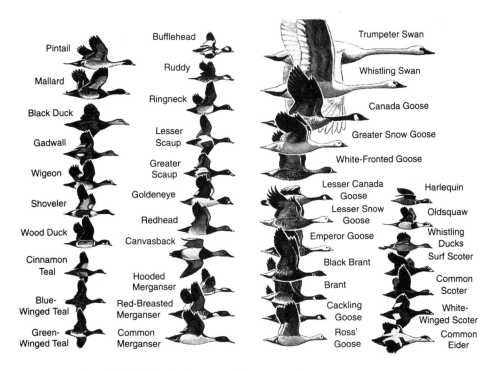

Comparative sizes of waterfowl. All birds in this illustration are drawn to same scale.

How to Use this Section

In addition to written descriptions and the natural history of North American duck and goose species, look for corresponding photographs of each bird in the color identification section. To verify a particular species' range throughout North America, see distribution maps accompanying text.

Dabbling Ducks

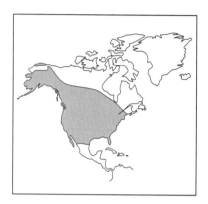

Distribution: Mallards are the most widely distributed duck in the Northern Hemisphere. More than half breed in the Prairie Pothole Country of the Dakotas and western Canada; the rest are found primarily in the Canadian parklands and subarctic deltas. Mallards will adjust their breeding range depending upon annual water and habitat conditions. More mallards migrate up and down the Mississippi Flyway than any other corridor, and nearly all North American mallards winter in the continental United States.

MALLARD
Anas platyrhynchos

OTHER NAMES: greenhead (drake); susie (hen)
LENGTH: 24 inches (drake); 23 inches (hen)
WEIGHT: 2½ pounds (drake); 2¼ pounds (hen)

ॐ

Identification from the blind: When flying, the mallard's white underwing feathers, predominantly white tail, and white borders of its blue wing speculum are its most distinguishing features.

In hand: Drakes sport a distinctive dark-green head, gray body, lavender breast, and narrow white neck ring, with orange legs and an olive-green bill. Hen has a dark-brown back, cream to tan underbelly, and orange and black bill.

Characteristics: Very vocal dabbling duck—especially the hen—found in flocks ranging from a handful to hundreds. Hens quack in a long, loud series; the drake's quack is low-pitched and raspy. The highly adaptable mallards—the most abundant wild duck in the world—thrive from city parks to the Canadian parklands. They feed on sedge seeds, grasses, smartweeds, and other aquatic plants, along with grains, often resting on flooded agricultural land during spring and fall migrations. Mallards are also among the first ducks to return to the breeding grounds each spring, having formed pair bonds in late fall and winter.

BLACK DUCK
Anas rubripes

OTHER NAMES: black mallard, red leg
LENGTH: 23 inches (drake); 20 inches (hen)
WEIGHT: 2¾ pounds (drake); 2½ pounds (hen)

❧

Identification from the blind: Similar in appearance and sound to the more common mallard. Plumage appears much darker than that of a hen mallard; in flight there are no distinguishing differences between hens and drakes. Black ducks can be easily confused with mottled ducks, but mottled ducks are seldom found north of Florida, Louisiana, and Texas.

In hand: Much darker plumage than a hen mallard, with a darker blue speculum. Adult drakes have yellow to pale-orange bills and reddish legs; hens sport olive-green bills and pink to red legs.

Characteristics: Black ducks are gregarious and commonly hybridize with mallards. Studies indicate that the expansion of mallards into the traditional black duck range may be contributing to the decline of black duck populations. Some biologists speculate that continued interbreeding may threaten the black duck's long-term genetic integrity. Though black ducks and mallards are close relatives, they are two distinct species.

Distribution: Black ducks are confined to eastern North America, with nearly twice as many of the birds being found in the Atlantic Flyway as the Mississippi Flyway. Although growing numbers of beavers across southeastern Canada and the northeastern U. S. have increased breeding pond habitat for black ducks, populations have steadily declined. Some scientists speculate that acid rain may be adversely affecting black duck breeding success. Plans for massive hydroelectric dams across Quebec may also jeopardize the future survival of the species.

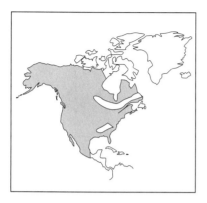

Distribution: Pintails are found across the Northern Hemisphere, covering more of the planet than any other species of waterfowl. Over half of all pintails on the continent winter in the Pacific Flyway; the species is most common west of a line from Michigan south to Mississippi. The Central Valley of California, a state that has lost more than 90 percent of its wetlands, is the largest pintail wintering area in North America. Some 15 percent of the continental pintail population winters in Mexico, predominantly along the west coast.

NORTHERN PINTAIL
Anas acuta acuta

OTHER NAMES: sprig, sprigtail, spike
LENGTH: 25 inches (drake); 21 inches (hen)
WEIGHT: 2¼ pounds (drake); 1¾ pounds (hen)

🦃

Identification from the blind: Sleek, long ducks with narrow wings, pointed tails, and exceptionally long necks. Drakes have white underparts, dark heads, and emit a trilling whistle. Hens are brownish and slightly smaller; the brown speculum has a noticeable white trailing edge. Hens have soft quacks, often a low croak when flushed.

In hand: Drakes, chocolate-brown head, throat, and back of neck, with thin white stripe up sides of neck; flanks, breast, and parts of the back are gray. The drakes' "sprig" consists of the two long black feathers that give the pintail its name. Hens are mottled brown with lighter underbelly. Drakes and hens have a blue-gray bill, but the hen's bill is duller.

Characteristics: Breeding pintails prefer short-grass prairie, and fly great distances to find the best nesting conditions. They return early in the spring to nesting grounds, and prefer the Prairie Pothole Country of the Dakotas and western Canada. Pintail populations fluctuate depending on the availability of water in this drought-plagued region. The future success of the species is directly linked to the integrity of their prairie breeding and nesting environment.

WOOD DUCK
Aix sponsa

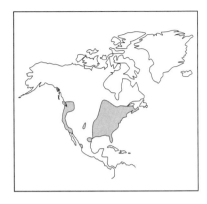

OTHER NAMES: Carolina duck, woodie, summer duck, squealer

LENGTH: 20 inches (drake); 19 inches (hen)

WEIGHT: 1½ pounds (drake); 1½ pounds (hen)

꙳

Identification from the blind: With its crested head, broad wings, protruding tail, and distinctive "wee-e-e-e-k, wee-e-e-e-k" call, wood ducks are among the easiest of all North American ducks to identify on the wing. In addition to their unique form, wood ducks have a noticeable white stripe along the back edge of their otherwise dark wings.

In hand: With its stunning iridescent blue-green crest, white throat stripes, reddish brown chest, and toffee sides, there's no mistaking the drake wood duck. The hen shares a similar conformation, but her drab brown plumage pales when compared with the drake.

Characteristics: By the turn of the century, wood duck populations declined steeply, in part from market gunning and unregulated hunting. In 1918, the Migratory Bird Treaty Act established fall hunting seasons, giving the species the chance to rebound. Wood duck populations have also benefited from the many thousands of artificial nest boxes that have been erected across the species' American breeding range. The birds prefer wooded river bottoms and flooded hardwood forests, where they commonly nest in tree cavities.

Distribution: The majority of the continent's wood ducks are found east of the Rocky Mountains. Most nest in the northern United States and southeastern Canada, wintering in the southeastern United States. Louisiana winters the largest number of wood ducks in the Mississippi Flyway, but Mississippi, Alabama, Arkansas, and Tennessee all play host to significant numbers.

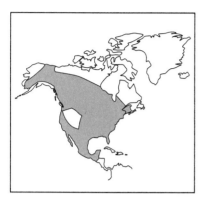

Distribution: Of all North American dabbling ducks, wigeon are one of the most northerly breeding species. Saskatchewan is home to the largest percentage of breeding wigeon; nearly 80 percent of the birds are produced in Canada. Most wigeon also winter in the Mississippi and Pacific flyways.

AMERICAN WIGEON
Anas americana

OTHER NAME: baldpate
LENGTH: 20 inches (drake); 19 inches (hen)
WEIGHT: 1¾ pounds (drake); 1½ pounds (hen)

Identification from the blind: Wigeon are relatively fast-flying birds with erratic flight patterns. A white shoulder bar is evident on drakes, and both sexes have telltale white underbellies framed by brown chest and flanks. The drake derives its "baldpate" moniker from its prominent white cap, apparent when the bird is fully plumed. Drake wigeon are vocal birds, with a whistle similar in sound to that made by pintails.

In hand: A black stripe separates the drake's white shoulder patch from the iridescent green speculum. Drakes also have a distinctive green stripe running from the eyes to the back of the head, and a thin black ring around the base of their bills.

Characteristics: Only blue-winged teal and pintails migrate southward before wigeon head to warmer climes; they begin their autumn trek as early as mid- to late August. Wigeon often inhabit semipermanent wetlands, and commonly bypass the Prairie Pothole Country in dry years, instead flying north to the Canadian parklands with its more consistently abundant water.

GADWALL
Anas strepera

OTHER NAME: gray duck
LENGTH: 20 inches (drake); 19 inches (hen)
WEIGHT: 2 pounds (drake); 1¾ pounds (hen)

❧

Identification from the blind: Both drake and hen feature dull white underwing and belly. Drakes have distinctive white-and-black speculums and russet shoulder feathers. Hens have smaller white wing patches and a generally mottled appearance, similar to hen mallards. Neither sex is considered vocal, but drakes occasionally voice a short "nyeck" and low-pitched whistle. Hens sound like a slightly higher-pitched hen mallard.

In hand: Drake gadwalls have relatively narrow gray-black bills; the hen's is yellow with black dots. Drakes have faded orange feet and legs; on hens they are yellow. The sides, back, and chest of drakes are gray, with a coal-black patch preceding the tail.

Characteristics: Gadwalls are late-spring migrants—one of the last species to arrive on the breeding grounds of the prairies of western Canada and the Dakotas. Where available, gadwalls prefer to nest on heavily vegetated islands. Gadwall ducklings are highly precocial, able to swim long distances shortly after hatching, which may be partly responsible for higher survival rates of gadwall ducklings compared with other puddle ducks. Gadwall populations are greatly influenced by the amount of water on their prairie breeding areas.

Distribution: Over three-fourths of the North American gadwall population winters in the Mississippi Flyway—primarily in the wetlands of Louisiana. The species is widespread across much of the Northern Hemisphere. Though the majority of the continent's gadwalls nest on the prairies, the birds have extended their breeding range eastward to include the Atlantic Flyway.

GREEN-WINGED TEAL

Anas crecca carolinensis

OTHER NAME: greenwing

LENGTH: 15 inches (drake);
    14 inches (hen)

WEIGHT: ¾ pound (drake);
    ¾ pound (hen)

Distribution: Three races of green-winged teal are found across the Northern Hemisphere. Roughly 15 percent of the birds in North America breed in Alaska and the Yukon's Old Crow Flats. The majority breed in the Northwest Territories and northern prairie Canada. Over half of the continental flock winters in the Mississippi Flyway—predominantly in the coastal marshes and rice sloughs of Louisiana and Texas. Some greenwings spend the winter as far south as Colombia, however.

Identification from the blind: Small, fast-flying duck, sometimes found in large flocks. Often swoops low over a marsh only to rise again in erratic, unpredictable flight. They feature a whitish underbelly, green speculum, and cream-colored bar at base of wing. Drakes are vocal, with a high-pitched "preep-preep," while hens often sound a sharp quack when startled.

In hand: Drakes are gray with a reddish brown head; a bright-green band beginning at the eye stretches across the head. Hens lack the prominent coloration of the drakes and have brown, mottled plumage. Both sexes have an unmistakable brilliant green speculum.

Characteristics: Greenwings are largely upland nesters, and are masters at concealing their nests. Brood survival is higher than most other dabbling ducks. They also migrate south much later than their bluewing brethren.

BLUE-WINGED TEAL

Anas discors

LENGTH: 16 inches (drake);
    15 inches (hen)

WEIGHT: 1 pound (drake);
    1 pound (hen)

Distribution: Breeds primarily in the U.S. and Canadian prairies and parklands. Most bluewings winter in Colombia and Venezuela, but some spend the winter on the Gulf Coast.

Identification from the blind: Small, fast-flying duck, typically seen in small flocks. Drake appears dark with pronounced white facial patch and white underwing, and has a faint "tsee-tsee" call; hens sport a high-pitched quack and have a white underwing similar to drakes, but with brown body plumage.

In hand: The drake's bill is black, the hen's grayish. The drake has a dark gray-blue head, white facial patch between eye and bill, black ventral region, and spotted sides and belly. Hens are similar but with more subdued coloration. Bluewings often resemble cinnamon teal during the fall, when both are in eclipse plumage. The wings of both drakes and hens have blue shoulder patches with green speculums.

Characteristics: Bluewings will fly north of their traditional breeding and nesting range in the Prairie Pothole Country if wetlands there are dry. They typically nest later than most puddle duck species. They are also among the first ducks to migrate south each fall.

CINNAMON TEAL
Anas cyanoptera septentrionalium

OTHER NAME: red teal
LENGTH: 16 inches (drake); 15½ inches (hen)
WEIGHT: ¾ pound (drake); ¾ pound (hen)

Distribution: Most cinnamon teal breed in the western United States, with about half found in Utah, according to annual surveys conducted by the U.S. Fish & Wildlife Service. Nearly all winter in the coastal marshes of Mexico and Central America.

Identification from the blind: Drakes appear especially dark in flight, with white underwing; hens are a drab brown. Both have a large, obvious blue shoulder patch.

In hand: Fully plumed drakes are a brilliant rusty red, easily distinguished from other teals. The drake's bill is black, and larger than that of other teals. The hen's bill is gray, with a light underbelly and dark-brown back. Both sexes sound similar to blue-winged teal.

Characteristics: Hybrids between cinnamon and blue-winged teal have become more common as the blue-wings expand their breeding range into traditional cinnamon teal nesting areas. Because the marshes adjacent to Utah's Great Salt Lake are vital breeding areas for cinnamon teal, many waterfowl biologists have encouraged the protection of these habitats. Cinnamon teal are early migrants, and prefer shallow wetlands rich in submerged aquatic plants.

Distribution: Shovelers commonly breed in the Canadian parklands and prairies of southern Canada and the Dakotas. Most winter in California, Texas, Louisiana, and Mexico, migrating through two major corridors between their breeding and wintering grounds from the Prairie Pothole Country of the northern United States and western Canada to as far as South America. The Klamath Basin in Oregon and marshes along the Great Salt Lake provide key stopover areas during migration.

NORTHERN SHOVELER
Anas clypeata

OTHER NAMES: spoonbill, spoony, smiling mallard, neighbor's mallard
LENGTH: 19 inches (drake); 18 inches (hen)
WEIGHT: 1½ pounds (drake); 1½ pounds (hen)

❧

Identification from the blind: Oversized bill and short tail make the shoveler's silhouette appear awkwardly front-loaded. Drakes have white underwings, dark head, and russet underbelly. Hens are drab brown with telltale spoonbill form. Both hen and drake are roughly midway in size between teal and mallards.

In hand: Drakes sport white breast, russet flanks, dark iridescent-green head and distinctive spoon-shaped bill. Hens are similar in form with brownish yellow bill and orange legs and feet.

Characteristics: Shovelers use their broad bills to filter crustaceans from the mud, relying entirely on animal food throughout their lives. This makes shovelers especially sensitive to chemical contaminants and wetland alterations that disturb sediments. Shovelers exhibit a strong homing tendency, most returning to the same nesting area they occupied the previous year.

MOTTLED DUCK
Anas fulvigula maculosa

OTHER NAMES: summer duck, black duck
LENGTH: 22½ inches (drake); 21 inches (hen)
WEIGHT: 2½ pounds (drake); 2⅓ pounds (hen)

ح&

Identification from the blind: As its name implies, the mottled duck sports drab brown plumage, and is virtually indistinguishable in flight from a hen mallard or Florida duck.

In hand: The mottled duck has a slightly darker tail than a hen mallard and faint white borders to speculum. It is not as dark as a black duck nor are its wings as large. The hen and drake are very similar in appearance, except that the drake has an olive bill while the hen has an orange-and-black bill; both have orange feet.

Characteristics: A mottled duck hen will renest up to five times if her nests are destroyed. Nesting success depends largely upon the availability of water along the U.S. Gulf Coast. They prefer to nest in thick stands of cordgrass in either fresh or slightly brackish water. Mottled ducks frequently breed with mallards; most recent research indicates that about 5 percent of Florida's mottled ducks exhibit mallard characteristics.

Distribution: There are two distinct breeding populations of mottled ducks: one in Florida and the other from Alabama west and south to the coastal areas south of Tampico, Mexico. Mottled ducks don't migrate to the extent of many of their North American brethren, but will move seasonally based on habitat conditions.

Distribution: Fulvous whistling ducks are found on four continents. In North America, most breed in Mexico, with lesser numbers nesting on the American Gulf Coast—in Texas, Louisiana, and California. Most of the birds winter in the same range they occupy when breeding; however, those in the United States fly south to the marshes of Tamaulipas, Mexico, to spend the winter.

Fulvous Whistling Duck
Dendrocygna bicolorhelva

OTHER NAMES: fulvous tree duck, Mexican squealer
LENGTH: 18 inches (drake); 17 inches (hen)
WEIGHT: 1¾ pounds (drake); 1½ pounds (hen)

Identification from the blind: These ducks appear unusually long in flight, with stretched necks and protruding, shorebirdlike legs. Drakes and hens look similar in flight, sharing tan heads and bellies with dark backs. They are also highly vocal birds, with a unique "kweeoo" whistle that carries over long distances.

In hand: Both sexes have black wings and tails with white rumps and flanks. Bills and feet of both drakes and hens are gray, and the iris is dark brown. Sides of neck are cream, with thin, dark striations.

Characteristics: Researchers suspect that fulvous whistling ducks mate for life, and it is not unusual for hens to lay large clutches of more than 20 eggs. Despite their common name "tree duck," they construct their nests on the ground using nearby vegetation—often in rice fields.

Diving Ducks

GREATER SCAUP
Aythya marila mariloides

OTHER NAMES: broadbill, bluebill
LENGTH: 18½ inches (drake); 17 inches (hen)
WEIGHT: 2¼ pounds (drake); 2 pounds (hen)

Identification from the blind: Greater scaup are found more often on coastal bays, sounds, and fjords than on the freshwater inland areas preferred by their lesser brethren. The two are often difficult to distinguish unless seen together, when the greater scaup's larger size is readily apparent. Hens are brown with cream-colored bellies and a white ring of plumage surrounding the base of the bill. Older hens also develop a white ear patch visible at a distance.

In hand: Both sexes have unusually wide bills; drakes have a dark head with a greenish cast. Drakes also have much whiter sides than lesser scaup. Both drakes and hens have gray bills, and gray legs and feet with darker nails. Drake's eyes are yellow, hen's are brown.

Characteristics: Greater scaup are more apt to breed their first year than are lesser scaup. Breeding as isolated pairs, they are partial to nesting in marshy tundra adjacent to open water. Greater scaup hens prefer nest sites with visibility in all directions.

Distribution: Greater scaup breed across both the arctic and subarctic regions of North America. About 75 percent of the continent's population breed in Alaska—the majority on the Yukon Delta. Though most greater scaup are produced in the Pacific Flyway, more than half of the continental population winters in the Atlantic Flyway from Maine to Cuba. The proliferation of European zebra mussels in the Great Lakes has led a growing number of diving ducks to stop and feed near Point Pelee in Lake Erie during their migratory travels.

Distribution: Lesser scaup breed from the Bering Sea in the northwest to the parklands of the northern United States. The majority winter in the coastal marshes of Louisiana; of all North American lesser scaup, 60 percent winter in the Mississippi Flyway—predominantly in the marshlands of Florida.

LESSER SCAUP
Aythya affinis

OTHER NAME: bluebill
LENGTH: 17 inches (drake); 16½ inches (hen)
WEIGHT: 1¾ pounds (drake); 1½ pounds (hen)

≈●

Identification from the blind: Scaup are often associated with the open water of large lakes or bays, where they may congregate in flocks numbering into the thousands. Drakes feature dark heads, chests, and rumps, and sport a rapid wing beat. They'll commonly approach decoys without circling, diving in rapid flight over the blocks. Their dark heads lead them to sometimes be mistaken for canvasbacks, but canvasbacks are considerably larger and have much lighter colored backs.

In hand: Drakes have a dark head with a purplish hue and a gray back, white sides, and yellow eyes. Hens have dark-brown backs, brown sides, white underbellies, and feature a white ring around the base of the bill.

Characteristics: Lesser scaup hens seldom breed before the age of two years. Older hens are more likely to produce successful broods. Breeding scaup favor more permanent and deeper wetlands, where they can find vegetation over water in which to construct nests.

CANVASBACK
Aythya valisineria

OTHER NAME: can
LENGTH: 21 inches (drake); 20 inches (hen)
WEIGHT: 2¾ pounds (drake); 2½ pounds (hen)

ᏋᎲ

Identification from the blind: Canvasbacks are the fastest flyers of the large ducks, with an even-paced flight more akin to that of a mallard than to other diving ducks. With their large, dark heads, canvasbacks appear top-heavy in flight.

In hand: Drakes have a reddish brown head with a wide black collar at the base of the neck. The drake's back is light gray to white, as are the sides and belly. Both sexes sport a dark rump; drakes have blood-red eyes, while hen's are brown. Hens have tan heads, a dark brown chest, and cream sides and bellies. The bills of both are black, with gray-blue legs and feet.

Characteristics: Despite a long series of closed hunting seasons, populations of canvasbacks have not increased. The majority breed in the Prairie Pothole Country of the Dakotas and western Canada. Increases in populations of predators such as raccoons, and interference from parasitic redhead ducks have adversely affected canvasback populations.

Distribution: The highest concentrations of nesting canvasbacks occur in southwestern Manitoba. Though most canvasbacks once wintered in the Atlantic tidewaters, the loss of preferred aquatic plants such as wild celery has caused the birds to alter their migratory patterns. In the Atlantic Flyway, many cans have abandoned Chesapeake Bay in favor of North Carolina's Pamlico Sound. Catahoula Lake in Louisiana now holds the greatest concentrations of wintering canvasbacks in the world.

Distribution: Most redheads breed in the continental United States, favoring the Prairie Pothole Country of the Dakotas and marshes of the intermountain West. Sizable numbers, however, breed on the Athabasca and Saskatchewan river deltas of Canada. Some 80 percent of all redheads winter along the Gulf Coast from Florida to the Yucatan Peninsula, with the greatest concentration on the Laguna Madre of Texas.

REDHEAD
Aythya americana

OTHER NAME: pochard
LENGTH: 20 inches (drake); 19 inches (hen)
WEIGHT: 2½ pounds (drake); 2 pounds (hen)

Identification from the blind: In flight, the redhead's silhouette is similar to a mallard's; the redhead's coloration closely resembles that of canvasbacks. Redheads lack the rapid wing beats common to other diving ducks, but their flapping motion is noticeably faster than that of mallards.

In hand: Drakes have bulbous red heads and necks, black chest collars, and gray backs and sides. Drakes also have yellow eyes—not red like a drake canvasback—and sport a two-toned bill. Hens have a tan head and neck, and a brown chest with cream back and sides.

Characteristics: Redhead hens frequently lay their eggs in the nests of other redheads and even other duck species. When the ducklings hatch, the host hen raises the birds. However, not all redhead hens are parasitic.

RING-NECKED DUCK
Aythya collaris

OTHER NAMES: ringbill, blackjack
LENGTH: 17 inches (drake); 16½ inches (hen)
WEIGHT: 1¾ pounds (drake); 1½ pounds (hen)

Identification from the blind: Though ringnecks appear similar to scaup, they tend to be found on smaller bodies of water, such as wooded potholes, bottomland ponds, and tree-lined marshes. Drake ringnecks have dark wings, and a black head, chest, and tail, and both sexes fly rapidly and erratically. Hens have dark-brown backs, chest, and sides with tan underbellies.

In hand: The drake's faint brown neck ring is only visible up close. Drakes also have a distinctive white ring framing the black nail of their bills, and bright yellow eyes. Hens appear markedly more drab, with a less prominent white bill ring than the drake's.

Characteristics: Acid rain is thought to be affecting ringneck populations in the northeastern United States. Duckling survival on more acidic lakes has been lower than on waters with a higher pH. Ringnecks prefer to nest over water, especially those waters surrounded by woodlands.

Distribution: The majority of the continent's ringnecks breed in northern Alberta, Saskatchewan, and Manitoba. More than 90 percent of the entire continental population is found in the eastern U.S. Of those wintering in the Atlantic Flyway, more than 50 percent are found in Florida—especially in the vicinity of Lake Okeechobee.

Distribution: Common goldeneyes are found across North America, Europe, and Asia; their North American breeding area ranges from Alaska to Newfoundland. More than half of the continent's wintering goldeneyes are found on the Pacific Coast from Alaska to Washington. More than 30 percent of the birds are found on the Atlantic Coast, and the remainder congregate predominantly in the Great Lakes region during winter.

COMMON GOLDENEYE
Bucephala clangula americana

OTHER NAME: whistler
LENGTH: 19 inches (drake); 17 inches (hen)
WEIGHT: 2½ pounds (drake); 1¾ pounds (hen)

Identification from the blind: Common goldeneyes are easily distinguished in flight by their wings' distinctive whistling sound—much louder than other ducks passing overhead. Common goldeneyes are relatively large diving ducks, with blue-black heads, white breasts, and a telltale white patch on the wings. Drakes also have a noticeable white spot in front of their eyes.

In hand: Common goldeneyes appear similar to Barrow's goldeneyes, but Barrow's are larger and have facial crescents instead of round patches. The common goldeneye has a large white wing patch separated by two dark horizontal lines. The wing patch on Barrow's goldeneyes sports only one dark line. Hens have dark-brown heads, white throat patch, and brown sides. Drake has bright-yellow eyes, the hen a pale-yellow iris. Both sexes have yellowish feet and legs, and gray-black bills.

Characteristics: Goldeneyes typically nest in tree cavities and thus enjoy a higher nest survival rate than ground-nesting ducks. They are also one of the last ducks to migrate south each autumn. Biologists are concerned that goldeneye wintering areas near coastal shipping lanes are vulnerable to oil and chemical spills, which could prove disastrous for the species.

BARROW'S GOLDENEYE
Bucephala islandica

OTHER NAMES: Rocky Mountain whistler, whistler
LENGTH: 19 inches (drake); 17 inches (hen)
WEIGHT: 2 pounds (drake); 1½ pounds (hen)

Identification from the blind: Drakes have dark heads, white underbellies, and a white patch on the wings. Hens feature dark-brown heads, lighter brown back and sides, and large white wing patches. Barrow's goldeneyes are big diving ducks with large, sloping heads.

In hand: Fully feathered drakes are easily distinguished from common goldeneyes by their larger size and crescent-shaped facial patch. The drake also has bright-yellow eyes, yellow legs, and a gray-black bill. The hen has yellow eyes, feet, and bill.

Characteristics: Barrow's goldeneyes, like their common goldeneye cousins, are cavity-nesting ducks that nest in trees, nest boxes, and even dens in the ground. The hens show a great deal of loyalty to previous nesting sites, returning to them each year so long as they remain viable.

Distribution: Barrow's goldeneyes are found from Alaska to Iceland; most breed in the intermountain regions of western Alaska and Canada. The birds' breeding range also extends as far south as northern California and Wyoming. Barrow's goldeneyes in the west winter from the Aleutian islands in Alaska to the coastal waters as far south as central California. The eastern population winters along the northern reaches of the Atlantic seaboard.

Distribution: More than 80 percent of ruddy ducks breed across the northern prairies of North America; lesser numbers nest in the intermountain West. Over half the continental population winters in the Pacific coastal states—mostly California—and along Mexico's western coast.

RUDDY DUCK
Oxyura jamaicensis rubida

OTHER NAMES: butterball, bull-necked teal
LENGTH: 15½ inches (drake); 15 inches (hen)
WEIGHT: 1⅕ pounds (drake); 1⅕ pounds (hen)

Identification from the blind: These small, stout ducks fly low over the water with rapid wing beats. They often prefer to escape from predators and hunters by diving, flying only as a last resort. While on the water, many drakes erect their fan-shaped tails at a 45-degree angle. Throughout the autumn and winter, both sexes wear drab gray-brown plumage.

In hand: In spring, drakes develop pronounced white cheek patch with a black head cap and reddish back and sides. The drake's bill also turns from gray-black in the fall to bright blue in spring; their tails protrude at a 90-degree angle during courtship. Hens in spring plumage have brown backs, white cheek patch, and dark-brown head caps.

Characteristics: Ruddy ducks prefer to feed on aquatic vegetation but will, on occasion, feed on crustaceans and other animal matter. Ruddy ducks are referred to as stiff-tailed ducks, for drakes often hold their tails erect and their tail feathers have rigid spines. Ruddy ducks also nest in emergent vegetation found in both large and small marshes. This species is further known for its parasitic behavior; hens often lay their eggs in the nests of other ruddy ducks and even other species. Despite their tiny size, ruddy ducks lay eggs larger than those of canvasbacks.

BUFFLEHEAD
Bucephala albeola

OTHER NAMES: butterball, dipper
LENGTH: 15 inches (drake); 13 inches (hen)
WEIGHT: 1 pound (drake); ¾ pound (hen)

ॐ

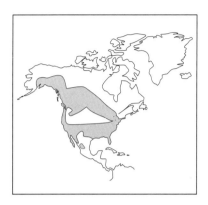

Distribution: Buffleheads are only found in North America, and breed from eastern Quebec to southern Alaska. Buffleheads winter along both coasts: from Maine to Florida in the east and from Washington to southern California in the West.

Identification from the blind: A small, fast-flying diving duck that appears black and white in flight. The drake has a large, wedge-shaped patch of white on its head—considerably larger than the white spot found on goldeneyes—a white chest, belly, and wing patch. Back and primaries are blue-black. The hen has a less-pronounced, smaller white head patch, and mostly brown head and wings. Flanks and tail are tan with lighter underbelly.

In hand: This tiny duck is one of the smallest waterfowl in North America. The drake has a disproportionately large, puffy head with iridescent dark blue-green plumage and large white patch. Both sexes have blue-gray bills, but the drake has pink legs and feet, the hen has grayish legs and feet.

Characteristics: Buffleheads are cavity-nesting ducks that first nest during their second year—often returning to the same nesting sites year after year. Nesting success can suffer from competition with other cavity nesters, such as squirrels, flickers, swallows, and goldeneyes.

Sea Ducks

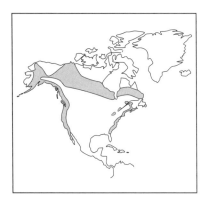

Distribution: Unlike other scoters, the surf scoter is the only scoter found solely in North America. They breed across the northern regions of Canada and winter along both Pacific and Atlantic coasts.

SURF SCOTER
Melanitta perspicillata

OTHER NAMES: skunkhead, sea coot
LENGTH: 20 inches (drake); 19 inches (hen)
WEIGHT: 2⅕ pounds (drake); 2 pounds (hen)

ଈ

Identification from the blind: This jet-black sea duck has small white patches on the back of its neck and on the forehead. The hen lacks the forehead patch, and the neck spot appears faded compared with the drake's.

In hand: The drake has a distinctive white, orange, and black shovel-shaped bill, with red legs and white eyes. The hen has a gray-black bill, yellow legs, and dark eyes.

Characteristics: Because these sea ducks winter in coastal waters subject to barge traffic, they are vulnerable to oil spills. Mollusks, barnacles, crabs, and other marine animal life comprise the bulk of the surf scoter's diet. Very little research has been conducted on surf scoters, and scientists still know relatively little about their biology.

BLACK SCOTER
Melanitta nigra americana

OTHER NAMES: American scoter, common scoter, black coot

LENGTH: 20 inches (drake); 18½ inches (hen)

WEIGHT: 2½ pounds (drake); 2 pounds (hen)

Identification from the blind: Other than a yellow spot on the top of the bill and gray underwings, the drake black scoter is, indeed, all black. The hen has a dark-brown skullcap with tan plumage below the eyes. Back, wings, and sides of the hen are all brown.

In hand: Both sexes have dusky gray feet; tails are wedge-shaped, longer than those of other scoters. Legs and feet of both sexes are gray-black; the iris is dark brown.

Characteristics: Like other scoters, the black scoter feeds almost entirely on animal life: barnacles, claw shrimp, mollusks, blue mussels, clams, oysters, and other crustaceans. The black scoter is also common to Eurasia.

Distribution: Little is known about the breeding range of black scoters across North America. The species has been identified breeding from the Aleutian Islands to Kotzebue Sound and on the Yukon Delta, Bristol Bay, and the Seward Peninsula. The birds winter south from the Aleutians all the way to southern California. In the east, black scoters spend their winters from Nova Scotia to Florida—most gravitating to the coastal waters of Georgia.

Distribution: The white-winged scoter is found throughout northern latitudes of North America, Europe, and Asia. Those in North America breed from northern Alaska across western Canada to North Dakota. The birds winter along both the Atlantic and Pacific coasts—in the west from southern Alaska all the way to Baja California, Mexico; in the east, from the Maritime Provinces south to coastal waters of North Carolina.

WHITE-WINGED SCOTER
Melanitta fusca deglandi

OTHER NAMES: sea coot, velvet scoter, whitewing
LENGTH: 21½ inches (drake); 20½ inches (hen)
WEIGHT: 3½ pounds (drake); 2½ pounds (hen)

Identification from the blind: These are the largest of the scoters, and typically fly low to the water in an undulating line. They appear coal black with the exception of a large white wing speculum—hence their common name.

In hand: The drake of this large, plump sea duck has a small white eye mask, a dark knob at the base of a yellow-orange bill, and dark-brown sides. Both sexes have pink feet. The hen has dusky brown plumage with small white cheek and ear patches. Hen lacks pronounced knob on its gray-black bill.

Characteristics: White-winged scoters do not breed until they are at least two years old—many not until age three. They were commonly found across the southern prairies of North America prior to 1950. Disturbance to lakes used for nesting probably led to their decline in those areas. White-winged scoters are late nesters, favoring wooded islands in permanent lakes. They feed primarily on marine animal life: mollusks, clams, mussels, oysters, scallops, crabs, crayfish, and barnacles.

KING EIDER
Somateria spectabilis

LENGTH: 23 inches (drake);
   21 inches (hen)

WEIGHT: 3¾ pounds (drake);
   3½ pounds (hen)

Distribution: King eiders are circumpolar arctic nesters, breeding from Siberia in the west to Ungava Bay in the east. They winter as far north as weather will permit. Most eastern kings winter along the coasts of New Brunswick and Nova Scotia, while those in the west typically remain along the Alaska Peninsula and Aleutian Islands, seldom venturing farther south than the Kenai Peninsula.

Identification from the blind: A large sea duck with a sloping bill and an orange knoblike protrusion at its base. Drake has whitish head, chest, and underwings; its black body has white patches above the speculum and at the base of the tail. The hen is uniformly brown with white underwings and slightly darker shades covering the outer primaries.

In hand: The white chest, protruding orange knob, and feathery "horns" projecting from the back of the wings give the drake king eider an unmistakable appearance. Both sexes have dark eyes; hens have dark olive-gray bills and feet.

Characteristics: Hen king eiders typically do not breed until they are at least two years old; the clutch is small—seldom larger than six eggs. Because king eiders nest so far north, their reproductive success is especially dependent upon spring weather conditions. Potential threats to future king eider populations include oil spills in the Beaufort Sea, as well as hydroelectric development in the Hudson Bay region.

COMMON EIDER
Somateria mollissima

LENGTH: 24 inches (drake);
   23 inches (hen)

WEIGHT: 4¼ pounds (drake);
   3½ pounds (hen)

Distribution: Different races of common eiders breed from Labrador in the east to the Bering Sea in the west. They winter from the southwest coast of Alaska south to the coast of British Columbia. In the east, the birds winter from the coastal waters of the Maritime provinces to New England.

Identification from the blind: These are the largest ducks in North America. In flight, they cruise in low lines over the water. Four races fall under the category of common eider, the differences in appearance being in weight and minor color changes. The drake has a black eye mask, white chest and back, and black sides, tail, and belly. In both sexes, the head appears V-shaped with protruding bill. Hens are a uniform drab brown.

In hand: Common eiders have more white on the back of their wings than do king eiders, and lack the fleshy knob on the bill. Both sexes have dark eyes; the drake has an olive-gray bill and feet, the hen a gray bill and feet.

Characteristics: Common eiders frequently nest near coastal shores on or near rocky ledges and islands. Hens normally return to the same nest site year after year, and do not breed until they are three years old. Clutches are typically small, averaging about four eggs per nest. Mussels, crabs, and other animal life comprise the bulk of common eider diets.

Distribution: There are two distinct populations of harlequins in North America. The Atlantic population breeds in Iceland, Greenland, Labrador, Baffin Island, and northeastern Quebec. They winter down the Atlantic Coast as far south as Virginia. Harlequin populations in the East have plummeted over the last two decades, and they are now listed as endangered. The birds are far more abundant in the west, where they nest from Siberia to Alaska and down the coast to Oregon.

HARLEQUIN DUCK
Histrionicus histrionicus

LENGTH: 17 inches (drake); 16 inches (hen)
WEIGHT: 1½ pounds (drake); 1¼ pounds (hen)

ð

Identification from the blind: Small, dark ducks with rapid wing beats, typically flying in small flocks. Few of the drake's colorful markings are visible from a distance.

In hand: With the possible exception of the drake wood duck, no other North American duck rivals the stunning coloration of harlequin drakes. Most of the drake's body is slate gray-blue, with distinctive white bars on the face, back of the head, neck, and sides of the chest. Its sides are rusty red, and it has small white spots over the ears. The hen is predominantly dark brown, with white ear and chin patches.

Characteristics: Though most harlequins winter in coastal bays and inlets, the majority move inland to nest along mountain streams, favoring rocky shores. This makes them especially sensitive to logging and mining operations that alter stream ecology. Sexual maturation and breeding begin at age two; the relatively small clutches seldom exceed seven eggs.

OLDSQUAW
Clangula hyemalis

OTHER NAMES: long-tailed duck, sea pintail, cockertail
LENGTH: 21 inches (drake); 15½ inches (hen)
WEIGHT: 2 pounds (drake); 1¾ pounds (hen)

Identification from the blind: Oldsquaw drakes have a relatively long, slender body and two long, protruding tail feathers, which occasionally gets them confused with northern pintails. In winter, plumage on oldsquaw drake has much more white on its head, and a distinctive brown-black chest. In summer, the drake's head is mostly black, and its back is dark brown to black. The hen also has more white on its head in winter, and features dark head plumage in summer. This species is unique for its radical seasonal plumage changes.

In hand: Oldsquaws have rounded heads with short bills. The drake has gray legs and feet, and a black bill with a pink band running crosswise before the black nail. The hen also has gray legs and feet; the bill ranges from dark gray to bluish green.

Characteristics: Most oldsquaws do not breed until they are two or three years old; clutches are usually small. Despite this, they are probably the most abundant duck to nest in the high arctic. Scientists have estimated that there are upwards of 4 million oldsquaws in North America during a typical year. The bird prefers to nest in shrubby tundra vegetation.

Distribution: The oldsquaw, or long-tailed duck as it is known in Europe, breeds in the arctic of North America, Greenland, Iceland, northern Europe, and Asia. In North America, oldsquaws winter in coastal areas—predominantly in the west—from the southern coast of Alaska to northern California. In the east, they can be found wintering from the Maritime provinces as far south as North Carolina.

Geese

Distribution: The 11 subspecies of Canada geese are found across North America from Alaska to the Maritime provinces as far south as the Gulf Coast of Mexico. Resident (nonmigratory) populations of giant Canada geese have been established in several northern states where, in some instances, populations have grown to nuisance levels.

CANADA GOOSE
Branta canadensis

OTHER NAME: honker

ADULT WEIGHT: There are 11 subspecies of Canada geese ranging in size from the 3-pound cackling Canada goose to the giant Canada, which may reach 20 pounds.

Identification: Canada geese are most often identified first by their "her-onk" calls and next by their appearance. There is a wide variance in size among races, but they share gray bodies with black heads and white cheek and rump patches. The larger subspecies are easily identified by their sheer size and long necks.

Characteristics: Canada geese reliably follow traditional migratory routes between well-established breeding and wintering areas. Although they mate for life, if one of the pair dies the other will seek a new mate.

LESSER SNOW GOOSE

Anser c. caerulescens

OTHER NAMES: eaglehead, blue goose, wavie

LENGTH: 29 inches (male); 28 inches (female)

WEIGHT: 6 pounds (male); 5½ pounds (female)

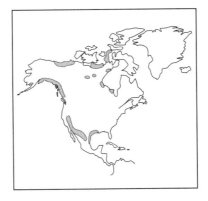

Distribution: These birds breed from northwestern Canada to Hudson Bay, and most migrate south from the Mississippi Flyway westward. Substantial numbers of lesser snows winter along the U.S. and Mexican Gulf Coast and as far west as the Central Valley of California.

Identification: Lesser snow geese occur in both white and dark color phases. White-phase birds are all white save for black wing tips, while dark or blue-phase snows range from gray to blue; adults may have white heads, necks, and partially white bellies.

Characteristics: As the most vocal of all North American geese, their cries can be deafening when the birds are concentrated on their wintering grounds. Lesser snow goose populations have grown substantially in recent years, to the point where the birds have degraded their own breeding grounds. Because of this, reproductive success has declined, and some biologists now warn that a population crash may be imminent.

GREATER SNOW GOOSE

Anser Caerulescens atlantica

OTHER NAME: wavie

LENGTH: 31 inches (male); 30 inches (female)

WEIGHT: 7½ pounds (male); 6 pounds (female)

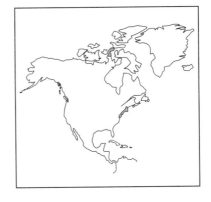

Distribution: Most greater snow geese nest off the northeast coast of Baffin Island, Northwest Territories. Fewer birds nest in Greenland, one of the few waterfowl species found in North America to do so. Most greater snows winter on the Atlantic Coast, from New Jersey to North Carolina.

Identification: Unlike lesser snow geese, there is no blue phase in greater snow geese; in appearance they are like larger versions of white-phase lesser snow geese, with the same high-pitched "la-luk" call. The birds are all white save for black wing tips, and sport ruffled neck feathers that run in ridges down the sides of the neck. Unlike the much smaller Ross' geese, snows have no barnaclelike growths at the base of their bills.

Characteristics: Breeding greater snow geese leave flocks of nonbreeding birds to establish nest sites on the tops of small scrub-covered hills nearby coastal waters. These birds commonly migrate at altitudes above 2,000 feet inflocks of up to 400 birds.

WHITE-FRONTED GOOSE
Anser albifrons frontalis

Distribution: Alaska and the western half of northern Canada are the major breeding grounds for white-fronted geese across the continent. Many birds winter in California's Central Valley, the Gulf Coast of Texas, and Mexico. Few birds are found east of the Mississippi River.

OTHER NAMES: specklebelly, spec, squeaker
LENGTH: 29 inches (male); 27 inches (female)
WEIGHT: 6⅓ pounds (male); 6 pounds (female)

ॐ

Identification: White-fronts appear dark in flight, sometimes confused with Canada geese at long distance because of their similar white ventral region and black tail. Adults have a white face ring around the bill and dark-brown blotches on their otherwise tan-gray underbellies. Juveniles lack both the white face and dark spots on the belly. They are very vocal geese, with a distinctive squeakie "otta-luk" cackle.

Characteristics: Prefers to breed on tundra lowlands, often adjacent to lakes or rivers. Usually does not breed until three years of age. Unlike many arctic nesting geese, white-fronts do not nest in colonies, preferring instead to spread out across the tundra. White-fronts are fond of rice, and have benefited from the proliferation of this rich food source across their U.S. wintering ranges.

Ross' Goose
Anser rossii

OTHER NAMES: little wavie, warty-nosed wavie
LENGTH: 25 inches (male); 23 inches (female)
WEIGHT: 4 pounds (male); 3½ pounds (female)

ॐ

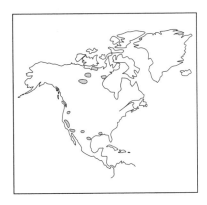

Distribution: Ross' geese nest in the central Canadian arctic and, to a lesser extent, on the tundra regions west of Hudson Bay. The birds winter from the Central Valley of California to New Mexico, the Gulf Coast of Texas, and central Mexico.

Identification from the blind: The Ross' goose is often confused with the snow goose, but it is considerably smaller than either the greater or lesser snow goose. Like the snow goose, the Ross' goose has black wing tips, but has a much shorter neck. There are also no blue color phases among Ross' geese.

In hand: The bill is considerably shorter than that of the snow goose, and often has wartlike growths around its base. Adult Ross' geese have pink legs and feet, while snow geese have red legs and feet.

Characteristics: This small relative of the snow goose is the first goose to depart the arctic breeding grounds each autumn. They typically form pair bonds their second year, but don't normally breed until reaching the age of three. Like snow geese, Ross' geese are the beneficiaries of increased grain production along the course of their North American migratory route, finding an abundance of spilled wheat, corn, and rice on which to feed.

ATLANTIC BRANT
Branta bernicla hrota

OTHER NAMES: brent goose,
   sea goose, white-bellied goose
LENGTH: 24 inches (male);
   23 inches (female)
WEIGHT: 3½ pounds (male);
   3 pounds (female)

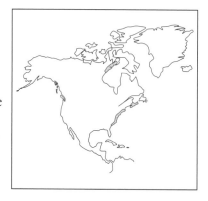

Distribution: Atlantic brant breed from Europe to the east coast of Canada. In North America, their primary breeding areas include Southampton, North Spicer, Air Force, Baffin, and Prince Charles islands. They winter from coastal New England to Virginia and North Carolina.

Identification from the blind: Despite its nickname "sea goose," the brant's long wings, short neck, and stubby body make it appear more ducklike than gooselike in flight. The Atlantic brant, while dark from the chest forward, is light gray to white behind the chest. It appears much lighter than its Pacific cousin.

In hand: It's difficult to distinguish between sexes in brant, as both have white chevrons behind each ear on the upper neck. Legs and bills of both sexes are black.

Characteristics: Spring weather conditions and the availability of water are the two key factors influencing Atlantic brant populations. The most ominous threat they face is the massive hydroelectric project slated for Quebec. Scientists believe this could alter the salinity of coastal waters along James Bay, affecting the vast eelgrass beds upon which brant depend for food.

BLACK BRANT
Branta Bernicla nigricans

OTHER NAMES: Pacific brant, brent
   goose, sea goose
LENGTH: 25 inches (male);
   23 inches (female)
WEIGHT: 3¼ pounds (male);
   3 pounds (female)

Distribution: Black brant nest along coastal Alaska and migrate south to winter from the coast of central California to the Baja California Peninsula. Lesser numbers of black brant winter along the coast of Sonora, Mexico, where water quality and the eelgrass beds upon which brant feed remain less affected by pollution.

Identification from the blind: Short-necked sea goose that appears gray-black save for its white rump. Difficult to distinguish in flight from Atlantic brant, but because ranges don't overlap, there is little confusion.

In hand: Both males and females are similar in appearance: black head, chest, and back; short black bill, black feet; and relatively long, slender wings in relation to its stout body and short neck.

Characteristics: Black brant are arctic nesters, and nest success is especially dependent upon weather conditions. They are subject to predation from arctic foxes, whose populations fluctuate. Brant eggs are also collected by native peoples. Black brant wintering areas are threatened by human encroachment and pollution of vital bays and estuaries, which has caused a decline in plant species upon which brant depend.

DABBLING DUCKS

MALLARD

Hen (left); Drake
Scott Nielsen

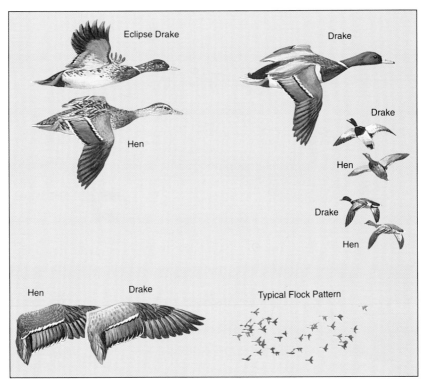

Illustration courtesy U.S. Fish & Wildlife Service

BLACK DUCK

Hen
Scott Nielsen

Eclipse Drake

Hen

Drake

Similar Sexes

Hen Drake

Typical Flock Pattern

Illustration courtesy U.S. Fish & Wildlife Service

Drake
Scott Nielsen

NORTHERN PINTAIL

Hen
Scott Nielsen

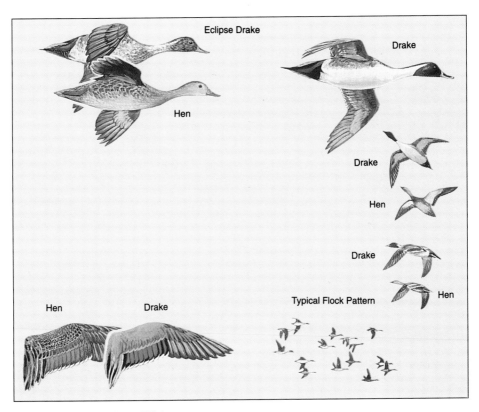

Illustration courtesy U.S. Fish & Wildlife Service

WOOD DUCK

Hen (left); Drake
Scott Nielsen

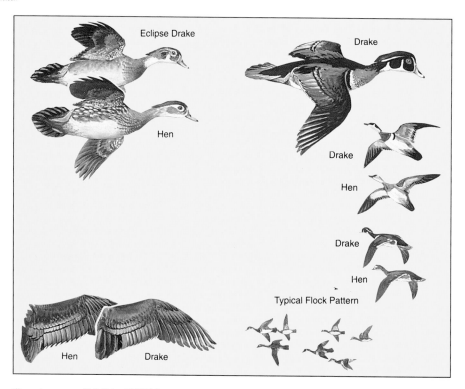

Illustration courtesy U.S. Fish & Wildlife Service

AMERICAN WIGEON

Drake (left); Hen
Scott Nielsen

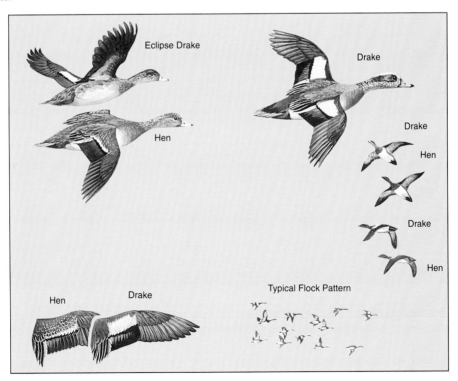

Eclipse Drake

Hen

Drake

Drake

Hen

Drake

Hen

Hen   Drake

Typical Flock Pattern

Illustration courtesy U.S. Fish & Wildlife Service

Hen (left); Drake

Scott Nielsen

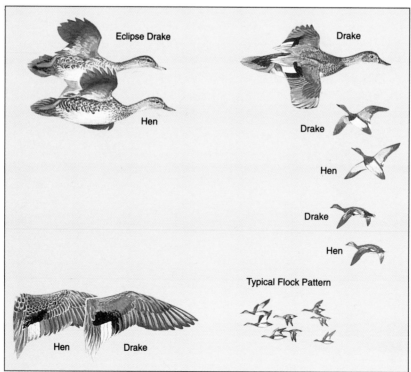

Eclipse Drake

Hen

Drake

Drake

Hen

Drake

Hen

Typical Flock Pattern

Hen   Drake

Illustration courtesy U.S. Fish & Wildlife Service

Drake
Scott Nielsen

Hen
Scott Nielsen

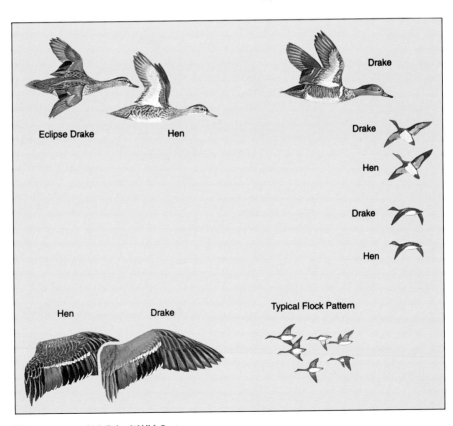

Eclipse Drake

Hen

Drake

Drake

Hen

Drake

Hen

Hen

Drake

Typical Flock Pattern

Illustration courtesy U.S. Fish & Wildlife Service

Drake
Scott Nielsen

BLUE-WINGED TEAL

Hen
Scott Nielsen

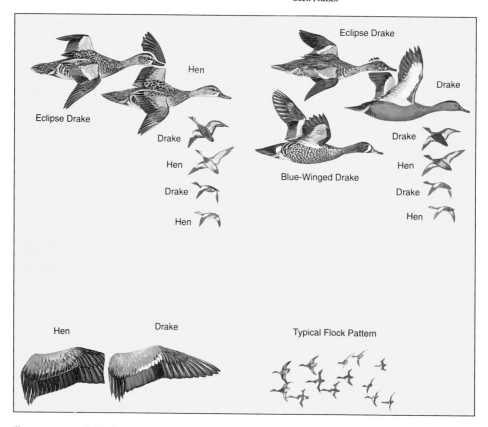

Illustration courtesy U.S. Fish & Wildlife Service

CINNAMON TEAL

Drake
Scott Nielsen

(*See previous page*)

Hen
Scott Nielsen

Hen; Drake
Scott Nielsen

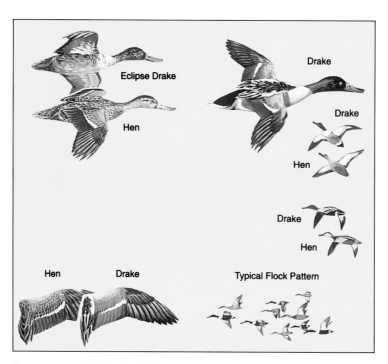

Illustration courtesy U.S. Fish & Wildlife Service

MOTTLED DUCK

Drake
Visuals Unlimited

FULVOUS WHISTLING DUCK

Sexes look alike
Scott Nielsen

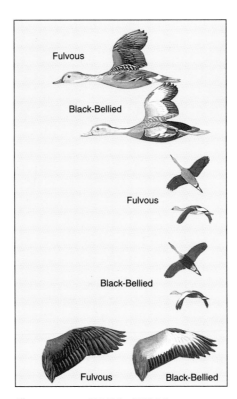

Fulvous

Black-Bellied

Fulvous

Black-Bellied

Fulvous   Black-Bellied

Illustration courtesy U.S. Fish & Wildlife Service

DIVING DUCKS

Hen
Scott Nielsen

GREATER SCAUP

Drake
Scott Nielsen

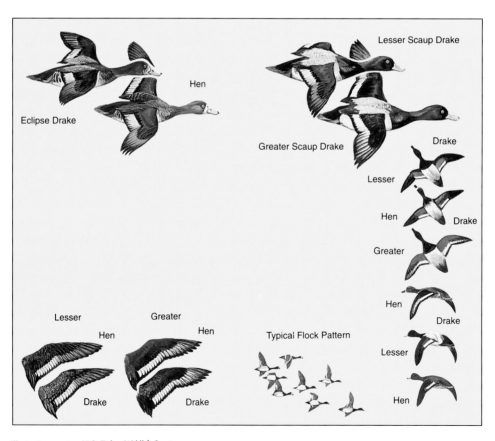

Lesser Scaup Drake

Hen

Eclipse Drake

Greater Scaup Drake

Drake

Lesser

Hen

Drake

Greater

Hen

Drake

Lesser

Hen

Lesser

Greater

Hen

Hen

Typical Flock Pattern

Drake

Drake

Lesser

Hen

Illustration courtesy U.S. Fish & Wildlife Service

LESSER SCAUP

Drake (left); Hen
Scott Nielsen

CANVASBACK

Hen
Scott Nielsen

Drake
Scott Nielsen

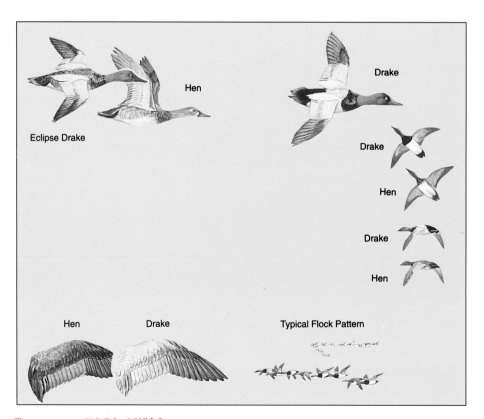

Eclipse Drake

Hen

Drake

Drake

Hen

Drake

Hen

Hen

Drake

Typical Flock Pattern

Illustration courtesy U.S. Fish & Wildlife Service

REDHEAD

Hen (left); Drake
Scott Nielsen

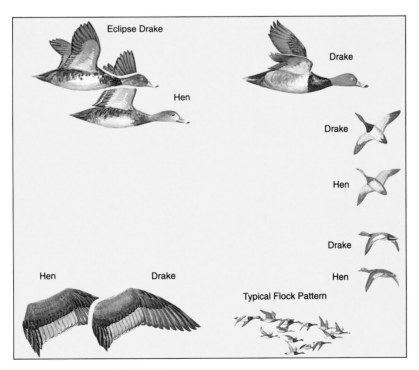

Illustration courtesy U.S. Fish & Wildlife Service

RING-NECKED DUCK

Drake (left); Hen
Scott Nielsen

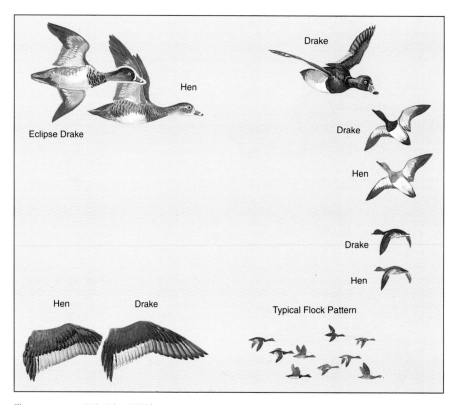

Eclipse Drake

Hen

Drake

Drake

Hen

Drake

Hen

Hen   Drake

Typical Flock Pattern

Illustration courtesy U.S. Fish & Wildlife Service

COMMON GOLDENEYE

Drake
Scott Nielsen

Hen
Scott Nielsen

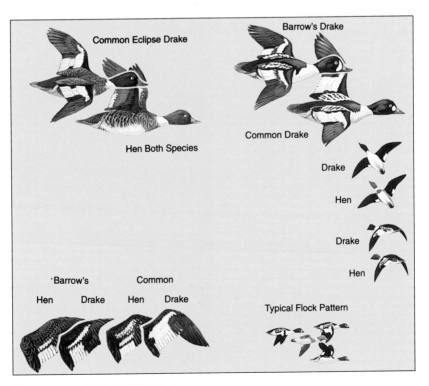

Common Eclipse Drake

Barrow's Drake

Hen Both Species

Common Drake

Drake

Hen

Drake

Hen

'Barrow's Common

Hen Drake Hen Drake

Typical Flock Pattern

Illustration courtesy U.S. Fish & Wildlife Service

BARROW'S GOLDENEYE

Drake
Leonard Lee Rue III

Hen
Scott Nielsen

RUDDY DUCK

Drake; Hen
Scott Nielsen

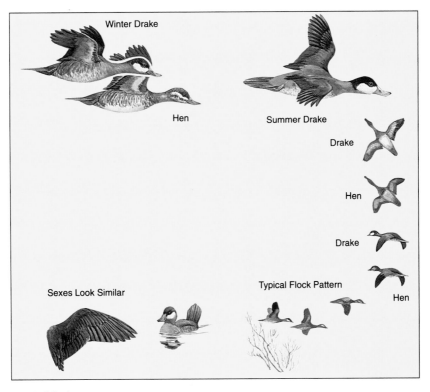

Winter Drake

Hen

Summer Drake

Drake

Hen

Drake

Hen

Sexes Look Similar

Typical Flock Pattern

Sexes Look Similar

Drake
Scott Nielsen

BUFFLEHEAD

Hen
Scott Nielsen

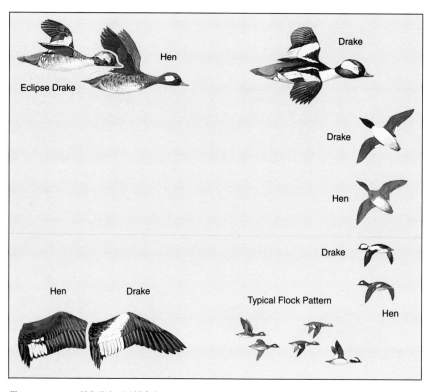

Illustration courtesy U.S. Fish & Wildlife Service

SEA DUCKS

SURF SCOTER

Drake
Visuals Unlimited

BLACK SCOTER

Hen (left); Drake (center)
Lon Lauber

WHITE-WINGED SCOTER

Drake
Lon Lauber

SURF SCOTER

Hen
Leonard Lee Rue III

Drake
Leonard Lee Rue III

Hen
Leonard Lee Rue III

COMMON EIDER

Drake (white); Hen (brown)
Leonard Lee Rue III

HARLEQUIN DUCK

Drake
John Hyde

Hen
John Hyde

Drake
Leonard Lee Rue III

Hen
Leonard Lee Rue III

GEESE

CANADA GOOSE

Sexes Look Similar
Scott Nielsen

LESSER SNOW GOOSE—BLUE PHASE

Blue Phase
Scott Nielsen

GREATER SNOW GOOSE—WHITE PHASE

White Phase
Scott Nielsen

WHITE-FRONTED GOOSE

Sexes Look Similar
Scott Nielsen

Sexes Look Similar
Scott Nielsen

Sexes Look Similar
Leonard Lee Rue III

BLACK BRANT

Sexes Look Similar
Len Rue, Jr.

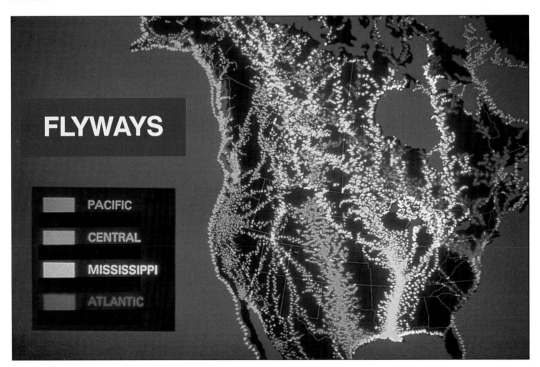

FLYWAYS

PACIFIC

CENTRAL

MISSISSIPPI

ATLANTIC

Four major North American waterfowl flyways
Illustration courtesy Ducks Unlimited

V

*B*oats and Blinds

If ducks or geese can be found on any given stretch of water, you can bet there's a boat, skiff, canoe, or pirogue that's been specially designed to carry hunters there. The evolution of waterfowling rigs from dories and sloops to modern craft constructed of space-age fibers has made it both easier and safer for hunters to reach their favorite gunning waters.

For many waterfowlers, their boat is a ticket to ever-changing hunting venues, for finding new gunning areas can be as simple as taking to water at a public boat launch and paddling, poling, punting, or motoring to a new locale. In many jurisdictions, it is perfectly legal to hunt a given body of water so long as you can gain access without crossing private land. Most river systems, streams, lakes, and even some marshes offer public-access hunting; check with law enforcement officials in your area for specifics.

Selecting the type of watercraft suited to your needs, then, is a matter of matching a boat to the waters upon which you intend to hunt. A big-water diver fowler will have different watercraft needs than, say, someone who plans to hunt mallards on a small cattail marsh. The following is a guide to waterfowling craft that can be used under a wide array of conditions.

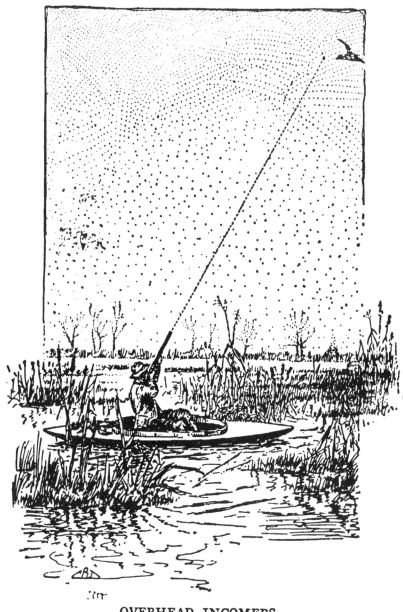

OVERHEAD INCOMERS

Illustration from American Duck, Goose & Brant Shooting, *1929.*

CANOES

Canoes have existed in one form or another since the beginning of recorded history. Their success is undoubtedly due to their versatility, for they can be used to hunt waterfowl on just about any type of water—except for large lakes or bays where waves may destabilize them. The term "canoe" stems from the Arawak language, the lexicon used by a tribe of people who inhabited the West Indies. Early canoes were typically fashioned from skins or bark, or were carved from logs, and were used to hunt, fish, explore new territory, and even wage war.

The forerunner of our modern hunting canoes was the creation of a Scotsman, John MacGregor, who built a craft he called the Rob Roy in the mid-1860s. A hybrid of Inuit design and European technology, these able, lightweight craft quickly gained widespread popularity and forever endeared the canoe to enthusiasts on both sides of the Atlantic.

Canoes offer waterfowlers a level of portability not found in most other craft. Today's canoes are made of tough, lightweight modern materials, such as Kevlar, polyethylene, fiberglass cloth, and Royalex. Aluminum canoes—first made as early as 1886—also remain in favor with many hunters because of their durability, though they are heavier than canoes made of the other materials. Because of a canoe's sleek, lightweight design, it doesn't take a trailer hitch to haul one around, and you don't need a drive-up boat launch to put-in.

Once on the water, canoes prove exceedingly maneuverable. While beaver dams, branches, and deadfalls may bar a hunter from taking a boat upstream, a canoe can be readily portaged around or over such obstacles.

For hunters who like the handling characteristics of a canoe but aren't particularly fond of paddling, there is the square-stern canoe. These are designed to be motor-driven and offer many of the advantages of small boats with the portability of a canoe. While canoes can be useful in many waterfowling venues, they do have limitations. Compared with many boats, they lack initial stability and payload capacity, and, except square-stern canoes, can only be propelled effi-

Canoes are age-old watercraft that owe their survival through the generations to their remarkable versatility.
Photo by Chris Dorsey.

Modern canoes, such as this one manufactured by Mad River, are often constructed of durable, yet lightweight material like Kevlar. Canoes continue to be popular with waterfowlers who value their maneuverability in shallow waters. Photo by Jim Henry, courtesy Mad River Canoe.

ciently by manpower (offset motor mounts are available for double-ended canoes but rarely prove satisfactory). If any of these characteristics make a canoe seem less than ideal, read on.

PIROGUES

If you're looking for a craft more stable than a canoe, don't look toward the pirogue. As Robert Ruark once wrote of the old-time dugouts, "A pirogue is a water-going ashtray that will capsize if you shave more closely on one side of the face than on the other."

While most hunters today think of pirogues as Cajun creations from the swamps of Louisiana, the term "pirogue" actually originates with the Carib Indians—a tough race of aboriginals who lived on small islands in the West Indies, traveling throughout the archipelago in hollowed-out logs.

Square-stern canoes offer many of the advantages of any other canoe, and give you the option of adding a motor to the crafts. This Manitoba outfitter finds such a boat the ideal choice when negotiating the small, rice-choked lakes of his area. Photo by Chris Dorsey.

This is a modern pirogue manufactured by Louisiana Pirogues. The craft is a distant relative of the sleek cypress dugouts once employed by Native Americans along the coastal wetlands of Louisiana. The trim pirogues move with ease through vegetation that would stall other boats. Photo by Joey Sedtal.

FETHERWATE DUCK BOATS

12 ft., (50 lbs.) $27.50 Mpls.

The construction is rigid, durable, tough and absolutely waterproof. Lighter than an average canoe. **De Luxe Model, with deck, $37.50.**

This ad appeared in Sports Afield prior to World War II, selling a "De Luxe (canoe) Model, with deck" for a mere $37.50.

North American Indians also used dugout canoes for transport, and Cajuns continued the practice, using cypress logs as the base wood of the thin craft. Modern pirogues are made of synthetic materials, and their sleek lines make them easy to paddle or pole through vegetation that would stop a larger craft in its tracks.

JOHNBOATS

Say "duck boat" to most waterfowlers and the image of a johnboat will come to mind. The wide, flat bottoms of these boats provide stable platforms from which to shoot, and they displace little water, making them ideal for operating in shallow areas. Like the canoe, the johnboat is another versatile craft that waterfowlers routinely use on everything from small streams to large lakes.

Johnboats like this one offered by Tracker Marine are versatile enough to use for both fishing and hunting. Many hunters construct blinds to fit on these boats or purchase blinds that are already assembled. Photo courtesy Tracker Marine.

Johnboats are fine platforms for outboard motors, so a hunter isn't limited to poling or paddling for locomotion. Johnboats come in many sizes, and their sturdy frames make them ideal for customizing; kits are available to help you do just that. Pop-up blinds that attach to johnboat frames are also available, helping you quickly transform the craft from a transport cruiser to a stable yet mobile hunting blind. Unlike permanent blinds, a mobile blind means you can always go to the ducks instead of trying the more difficult feat of coaxing them your way. If you choose to customize your johnboat, be sure to take advantage of the boat's large cargo space, but be sure to leave room for decoys, dogs, gear, and a hunting buddy.

Like canoes, johnboats can be purchased inexpensively and they transport easily—either in the back of a pickup or via a trailer. If you can afford only one duck boat, the johnboat is as versatile a craft as any.

LAYOUT BOATS

To meet the demands of turn-of-the-century epicures for canvasbacks and other big-water ducks, market gunners of the Atlantic tidewaters used layout boats to reach the large rafts of ducks that congregated on the deep bays. Sitting barely above the water's surface, these boats were usually positioned in the midst of enormous spreads of blocks.

Layout boats were typically one-man craft that were towed to deep water by a larger, more seaworthy boat. After positioning a generous spread of stool—big enough to lure ducks or brant away from nearby rafts of birds—one hunter would remain in the low-profile layout, which was anchored into position. An opening in the spread would be left in front of the boat to direct ducks to an area close enough to allow the gunner an easy shot.

The layout boat's low freeboard may have made them less visible to ducks, but it also made them vulnerable to heavy weather. That's why other hunters stood watch from a distance in the larger towboat. If the water got too rough or if it was time to rotate gunners, the larger boat would move in and the gunners could change places.

Notice the low profile of this One man Lay-Out Boat by Ron Bankes Marine Services. From a distance, the craft is almost undetectable in a decoy spread.

Though relatively few gunners continue to use this technique, some still cherish it as a venerable method of waterfowling, and some boatbuilders still build layout craft. Some modern layout boats—as is true of many of today's waterfowling craft—have injected-foam compartments to make them virtually unsinkable.

Other low-profile craft, such as sneakboxes, have been in use for more than 150 years. Probably the most famous, the fabled Barnegat Bay sneakbox, was the brainchild of Captain Hazelton Seaman, who designed and built his boat in 1836. Originally made of white cedar cut from the swamps of Seaman's native New Jersey, modern-day sneakboxes are available today built of fiberglass and aluminum. The mere fact that the boat is still in use today is testimony to its ingenious design.

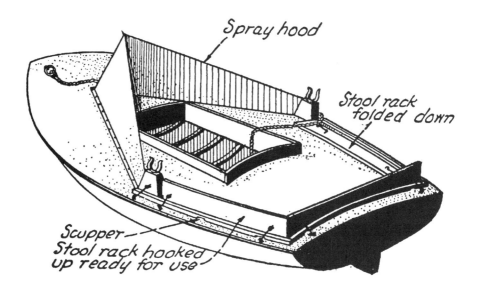

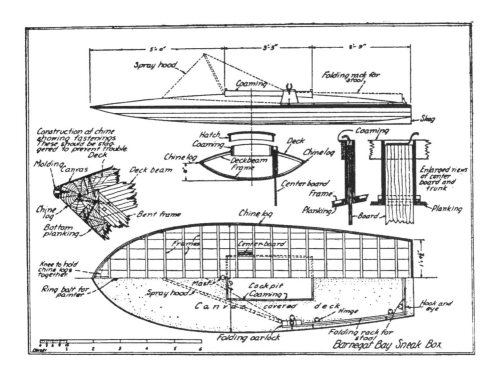

Illustrations from American Duck, Goose & Brant Shooting, *1929.*

The Phoenix Poke boat offers much of the maneuverability of a canoe with the stability of a johnboat. It is also an easy craft to conceal, which adds to its popularity among waterfowlers. Courtesy Phoenix Products.

SKIFFS

For many waterfowlers who spend the majority of their hunting hours in a small marsh where the waters are relatively calm, a skiff can be the perfect taxi from shore to blind and back. These light, portable, relatively inexpensive boats come in a variety of shapes and forms. The majority offer a bit more stability and cargo capacity than do most canoes. They are often ideal to paddle or pole through a marsh when jump-shooting, but if you plan to use them as a blind, be sure to tie them to stabilizing poles pushed into the mud on either side of the boat. These stakes will help keep the craft from tipping when occupants stand to shoot or when you send your retriever out to fetch a fallen bird.

BLIND LUCK

For some waterfowlers, a blind is a home away from home, a second house without the mortgage. I've been privileged to sit in blinds with piped-in gas heat and a stove, where a breakfast of eggs, bacon, and hashbrowns is served promptly at 7:30 each morning of the

The Porta-Bote, as its name implies, is designed to be a highly portable craft for wildfowlers. It is unique in that it folds for ease in transport.

waterfowl season. While there is something to be said for such amenities, such blinds are designed more for comfort than for practicality. In my experience, being able to change locations frequently is the key to getting ducks or geese consistently, for they are forever altering their daily feeding patterns. It doesn't take birds long to associate trouble

This Long Point Skiff is offered by Ron Bankes Marine Services, and has been modified to accept small motors. Like many modern waterfowling crafts, this skiff includes foam flotation for added safety.

with a permanent blind, so change venues if you want to keep surprising them.

A blind can be as simple as a piece of camouflaged cloth stretched over your body or as elaborate as a concrete bunker with swivel seats, shelves, and a telephone—yes, one blind out of which I hunted in Nebraska even sported a phone (heaven forbid not being able to order a pizza when the mood strikes).

When constructing a blind, remember that you'll need to be able to spy approaching birds without them seeing you. The most frequent mistake most hunters make is using vegetation or other blind material that doesn't match the surroundings. Disguising a marsh blind with brown cornstalks, for example, is as sensible as laying out a string of fluorescent decoys. Use the vegetation found in the immediate area of your blind; it's the only way to keep from being obvious.

Perhaps no other motor has done more to allow waterfowlers to access secluded waterfowl hideouts than has the Go-Devil, an ingeniously designed engine that allows hunters to travel through debris-infested waters. Here, the Go-Devil engine is pictured with an accompanying Go-Devil boat.

Address several questions when locating your blind: How many people will hunt from it? Will a separate entrance for a retriever be important? Is the area frequented by enough birds to warrant building a blind there? Should the blind be left open or covered? If covered, should you use sliding doors or the pop-up variety? Chairs or a bench?

If you decide to forgo a permanent blind in favor of more portability, choose materials that you can easily tote with you to the field or marsh. With the plethora of camo patterns on the market, it's easy to blend into almost any kind of cover, from cattails to cactus. A longtime friend of mine routinely carries six mallard decoys and a sheet of homemade camouflage that looks nearly identical to the matted rushes of a muskrat hut. He pitches his decoys in a pool adjacent to a muskrat house, stomps out a flat spot on the hut for him and his Lab to sit, drapes the sheet over the two of them, and waits like a praying mantis for the birds to approach within range.

This Canvasback boat is a creation of boat designer David Lee of Lee Boats. This deluxe model is a waterfowler's dream, offering plenty of storage compartments, built-in dog platform, stainless steel transom tie-downs, and anti-splash transom. It is made of fiberglass with a textured gelcoat finish. The craft can be used safely on big water and is equally effective in shallow water.

If it will go through water, wildfowlers will use it. This Arkansas hunter employs an all-terrain vehicle to get to and from his blind located in a flooded soybean field. Photo by Chris Dorsey.

Veteran New Jersey waterfowler Pete McLain is a strong advocate of coffin blinds, for they are both portable and effective in concealing hunters. He spends most of the duck season in the Prairie Pothole Country, and there is little cover near the small waters of the region. The low-profile blinds are a perfect choice for hunting in areas where cover is sparse—like a stubble field or a pond surrounded by short-grass prairie.

The best blinds are brushed with vegetation found immediately around them, for that is the only way to conceal your hide from the wary eyes of heavily hunted waterfowl. Photo by Chris Dorsey.

Essentially, a blind can be almost anything that conceals you from ducks or geese. Be creative. Round bales, pipe from a center pivot irrigation system, even a junk car along the edge of a field can be turned into a blind—nearly anything with which the birds are familiar. On one particularly memorable South Dakota goose hunt, geese from the Missouri River lifted off each morning and flocked by the thousands to the midst of an expansive, picked cornfield. The birds were

The virtue in constructing simple blinds is that you're not tied to the same hunting venue. Being able to relocate to match the movements of birds is the key to hunting success. Photo by Chuck Petrie.

too far from fence-lines or other cover to reach, so we decided to hide ourselves in two wooden calf crates that the farmer upon whose land we were hunting had left in the field. On schedule, the geese departed the river and flew directly toward our field, as they had been doing for two days. Some three hundred Canadas lighted near the four of us before we dropped the crate lids and took incoming birds at close range.

If you are hunting over water, try making a quick blind for your boat from local vegetation—it's far easier than building a permanent structure and likely more effective, too. No matter what kind of permanent or makeshift blind you use, pay attention to its position relative to the sun, prevailing winds, and even other blinds in the area. Bird movements often change when the first shot of the season is fired over the marsh, so don't go to great lengths to build a permanent blind be-

Almost anything can be modified to work as a blind. Here, the author takes a limit of Canada geese in a South Dakota cornfield by using a livestock crate as a hide. Photo by Chuck Petrie.

This sunken blind in the midst of California's famous Suisun Marsh looks like little more than a muskrat hut. Below the surface there is a comfortable place to sit, a safe gun rest, and a separate compartment for a retriever. Photo by Chris Dorsey.

fore you are reasonably certain you can predict bird patterns. Rising or falling water levels, nearby crop harvests, and local hunting pressure will all affect both the number of birds in the area and the direction from which they might approach.

If you are debating whether or not to build a permanent blind, remember that hot breakfast in the blind might sound appealing, but a limit of birds before breakfast is even better.

At right is an innovative bale blind built by noted decoy designer Darrel Wise. The blind features a unique roll-back cover that opens to allow hunters plenty of room to shoot. At left is one of the blinds concealed in straw to look like any other bale on the prairie. Photo by Darrel Wise.

VI

The Calling Edge

Perhaps nothing in the hunting world is as sweet as fooling game by mimicking its voice. For the waterfowler, success in calling is about more than just sounding like a duck or goose. It's a matter of knowing *when* to sound like them, choosing the right location from which to call, and, quite often, knowing how to match your calling with an alluring decoy presentation. An accomplished master of wildfowl calling also knows the best call for the moment, for—to paraphrase Mark

Calling waterfowl is about more than sounding like a duck or a goose—it's a matter of knowing when and how to blow the right call depending on the movements of the birds. Call guru David Hale is an expert at "reading" the body language of birds, hence his success in calling waterfowl. Photo by Chris Dorsey.

Twain—the difference between the right call and the nearly right call is the same as that between lightning and the lightning bug.

Even the most eloquent, convincing recital will have little effect if a caller is not located where ducks want to light. A great degree of the intrigue of waterfowling is trying to decipher what a duck or a goose is thinking, how it perceives its environment, and what makes one bird plunge headlong toward your decoys while another doesn't take a second glance. Inside the acorn-sized brain of a duck or goose lie many mysteries destined to remain unsolved, for the moment you are confident you can predict the actions of waterfowl, a flock will come along that defies all previous notions. Indeed, there are no rules to calling ducks and geese, only theories; the longer one spends pursuing waterfowl, the more numerous those hypotheses become.

In the hands of experienced hunters, though, a duck or goose call becomes a musical instrument, a perfect blending of function and artistry. No amount of written instruction will make a novice fluent in waterfowl communication, but a foundation of fundamental calling principles can help you break the language barrier.

<u>DUCK TALK</u>

Imagine yourself seated in your favorite duck blind. Ahead is a spread of decoys, and you await the first flight of the day. Suddenly, a high flock of mallards passes overhead, silhouetted against a starlit sky. This is the perfect time to greet them with what's called the *highball* or *hail* call. The highball is a loud, long series of quacks that develop almost a ringing sound, tapering off after several repetitions. Though there isn't a hen mallard alive that duplicates the volume of this call, it serves as an excellent attention-getter. World champion duck caller and call manufacturer Buck Gardner likens this call to flagging decoying geese. "A flag doesn't look like a goose," he admits, "but it does get geese to notice decoys from a long distance and the same is true of the highball."

While some callers pride themselves on their ability to rattle their blindmate's eardrums with a loud highball, distant ducks apparently do not find this call overbearing. In fact, a loud highball might be the only way to capture their attention. As a general rule, the higher the ducks are flying, the louder you will need to blow your highball. Ducks may not immediately respond to your 10- to 15-note highball, but look carefully for any deviation in their flight—a hint that your decoys have been spotted and the birds are thinking about examining them more closely. If the ducks do not tip their wings, vary their flight direction, or circle back for another pass, save your breath, as they have another destination in mind.

Outdoor writer Tom Huggler (left) receives duck calling instruction from 1959 World Champion Jim Fernandez of Sure-Shot Game Calls. In the background, Feather Flex's Dave Berkley looks on. The trio was part of an industry group assembled to test new waterfowling gear during a Texas duck and goose hunt. Photo by Chris Dorsey.

Should high-flying ducks break away from the flock to examine your stool, you will want to begin a series of six to eight hen quacks in different pitches to give the illusion that several ducks are calling. "Reading" a duck's in-flight attitude and behavior takes considerable experience, and only time in a blind observing how ducks respond to other ducks and to calling will give you an understanding of what to expect from the birds. Too many hunters hang up their calls at the end of each season, when they could be back in the marshes in the spring practicing their calling as the birds migrate north. If that isn't practical, try venturing to a local park where there might be a flock of resident mallards; study their behavior and practice your calling until you can closely mimic many of their calls.

With ducks approaching, you'll want to begin the *lonesome hen* call, a protracted series of quacks of similar tone and volume. This can be modified by faster repetitions to add a sense of pleading or urgency. This is the kind of call you have undoubtedly heard from hen mallards at your favorite marsh. While ducks are often looking for a place to feed, drakes are always looking for female companionship and can be especially receptive to a seductive rendition of the lonesome hen.

As ducks begin cupping their wings to set over your decoys, you'll want to blow an assurance call to encourage them to continue their flight path. Many waterfowlers use the *feed chuckle,* a rapid series of clucks sounding like a machine gun. Hen mallards seldom use this call, and ducks can quickly become suspicious of this unnatural sound if overused. Buck Gardner prefers to use a mixture of clucking sounds, which hens commonly make when they are resting contentedly on the water.

World champion caller Tim Gesch likes to make what he calls the barnyard hen sound when ducks begin approaching. This is a soft call somewhere between a squeak and a quack, a rendition you often hear

World champion duck caller Buck Gardner (right) demonstrates the nuances of proper duck and goose calling. Great callers are musicians of sorts, for they know how to play the right tune to lure birds to the gun. Photo Chris Dorsey.

hens making as you slip quietly into a predawn marsh. Gesch uses this call until the birds are over the decoys and he's ready to shoot.

When faced with ducks that repeatedly circle out of shotgun range, you'll need to change your calling cadence or do something different to convince the birds that it is, indeed, safe to land. Many hunters attach strings to their decoys so that they can tug on the blocks to give them movement on the water—a little edge that might be enough to coax skeptical ducks to light among the decoys.

Ducks that are reluctant to approach are often gun-shy from previous experiences with decoys. Remember that ducks—especially those that have made it south past a gauntlet of hunters in the northern ranges of a flyway—have often seen scores of decoy presentations and have undoubtedly gotten an earful of hunters blowing duck calls. To fool these birds, you need to approximate closely the natural sound of a duck and be careful not to move or make unnatural noises in the blind.

The larger an approaching flock of ducks, the more important it is to reduce your movement in the blind, for it takes but one duck to alert the entire flock to your presence. With so many eyes and ears looking and listening for danger, there is very little margin for error in your decoy presentation and calling. If ducks look like they are leaving the area, Gesch blows a more demanding call by speeding up the cadence and increasing the volume of his quacks. This is the *comeback* call, perhaps the most important call the duck hunter can master.

With time in the blind, you will develop the ability to interpret a duck's body language as it reacts to the various calls. Only through familiarity with these sounds will you be able to draw on a repertoire of calls that will help lure ducks to your blind. If the birds show little interest in your calling, don't be afraid to put your calls in your pocket, for perhaps the most important note a caller can strike is that of silence.

Most puddle duck species will respond to the mallard call, but there are several other calls that specifically mimic the sounds made by pintails, wood ducks, teal, wigeon, and gadwall. Scores of video and cassette tapes are available to waterfowlers who want to learn more

Several call makers offer pintail and wigeon whistles that can be used to help coax those birds over your decoys. Both species, however, readily respond to mallard calls as well. Photo by Scott Nielsen, courtesy Ducks Unlimited, Inc.

about calling ducks, but an even better source of instruction is an experienced caller who can tutor you in the field. If you lack a good place to hunt, improve your calling skills and you'll find yourself being invited to hunt many new locations, for there's always room in a blind for a quality caller.

BLOWING BASIC DUCK CALLS

Feed Chuckle: A rapid series of low grunting sounds, most commonly used as a confidence or assurance call. Rapidly repeat *tick-et, tick-et, tick-et* into your call to produce the feed chuckle. This call is most effective when mixed with soft clucks and quacks to convince skeptical birds to approach your decoys. To produce a quack, simply say the word *quit* into the call.

Comeback: An urgent-sounding series of quacks blown rapidly up and down the scale. This call is used to turn ducks that are moving away from your decoys.

Highball: A series of loud, long quacks that start high on the scale and taper off after several repetitions. This is used as an attention-getter when ducks are in the distance. The call consists of five or six quacks blown in increasingly shorter lengths: *quaaack, quaack, quack, quack, quack.*

Lonesome Hen: A protracted series of quacks, with tone and volume remaining the same. All other calls are a variation of this sound.

GOOSE TUNES

Like mallards, Canada geese are widely distributed, the most popular quarry of goose hunters across North America. They are also highly vocal birds that respond readily to calling. As is the case with ducks, to call geese successfully you must understand the synergy between calling, decoy placement, and location. The art of calling geese is an ancient one. Several tribes of North America's indigenous people still call geese with their voices. The first goose calls weren't in use in North America until almost half a century after the invention of the single-reed duck call—an indication of the stronger interest in mallard hunting.

Canada geese consistently use five readily identifiable calls. The *greeting*, or *hail*, call is used when honkers spot other geese in the distance—often several hundred yards away—and are attempting to get their attention. When calling geese from afar, it's important to use a call that has sufficient volume to reach distant birds—especially if conditions are windy. If geese are flying high with rapid wing beats, it will be very difficult to convince them to coast to your decoys. You are more likely to lure geese that aren't too high or that are only slightly flapping their wings. To blow the greeting call, say *to-wit, to-wit, to-wit* into your call. The "to" represents the *her* of the *her-ONK* sound made by Canadas. The louder "wit" part of the call is the accented *ONK.* Many Canada geese also make a low, growling sound. To mimic this, say *grrrit, grrrit, grrrit* into the call, varying the loudness until it closely approximates the sound made by the geese.

Illustration from American Duck Shooting, *1901.*

The *intermediate greeting* call is used when geese have broken away from the flock to take a closer look at your decoys. Here, you'll want to decrease your volume slightly while increasing the speed of the *to-wits* to achieve an excited tone. Again, this call can be modified to re-create a variety of varying sounds; just experiment with your call as you listen to live geese. There is simply no substitute for quality practice.

The *cluck*, or *feeding*, call is used as the geese are flying directly toward the decoys to examine them more closely. This is an excellent time to add the growling sound to your call, for this will mimic the raspy sound of feeding geese, whose throats are dry and whose crops are partially filled with corn or other grain. Shorten the *to-wit* series blown into the call to make the cluck. The *double-cluck* is simply a modification of the cluck. To blow it, say *twit-it* in a series that begins slowly but builds rapidly.

One of the most important calls is the *comeback*, meant to plead with geese to return for just one more look at your decoys. It's a long, single note with a lonesome, forlorn sound and is the ideal call to use when attempting to turn birds away from another hunter along a refuge boundary. Modify your *to-wit* in a slow series consisting of *to-wiiiit, to-wiiiit, to-wiiiit*.

The last call used frequently by Canadas is the *lay-down* call. This is designed to reassure the birds that they've made a good choice to land near your decoys. To blow the lay-down, stutter the *to-wit* calls in short, quick bursts of sound and add a growl to achieve the murmuring sound of geese feeding contentedly.

You won't always need to recite each of these calls, but having them in your repertoire may make the difference between getting birds within shotgun range and watching them sail to distant blinds. Knowing how and when to use each of these calls will heighten your waterfowling enjoyment, for you will have the satisfaction of interacting with the geese brought to the gun.

THREE TYPES OF GOOSE CALLS

Resonate Chamber: This is the most popular call because it is the easiest to operate and usually adequately loud; however, it lacks the tonal range of the flute call. The reed assembly of the resonate chamber is part of the call's stopper, which is fitted into the barrel. As the caller blows into the call, air pressure builds until there is enough to cause the reed to vibrate against the reed base's sounding surface, producing sound. If air is blown rapidly into the call, the reed will "break" (or, hold against the sounding surface without vibrating). This produces the higher *ONK* sound of the Canadas' *her-ONK* call.

Flute: P. S. Olt introduced the first flute call in 1954, the now famous Olt A-50. While more difficult to master, the flute call possesses a wide range of tones that can be used to replicate the many sounds of Canada geese. While the reed acts much as the reed assembly in a resonate chamber call, the caller must control air pressure within the call by cupping his hands over the end of the call and by raising his tongue to

There are scores of custom and manufactured duck and goose calls from which to choose. Champion caller Tim Gesch surveys a selection from the vast field. Photo by Chuck Petrie.

the roof of his mouth while exhaling. This causes a constriction in air-flow as air passes into the call and over the reed assembly to produce sound.

Tube: Though this is the simplest of all goose calls, it is the most difficult to learn to use. The tube call consists of little more than a tube fitted with a rubber diaphragm stretched over one end and held in place by a rubber band. The tube call lacks the volume of the other two calls, but legendary caller Harold Knight used one to win the world goose-calling championship.

Brenda Cahill, stepdaughter of legendary caller Chick Major, continues to make the dixie Mallard Calls that Chick made famous. Photo by Chris Dorsey.

Noted waterfowling historian and call maker Howard Harlan fashions his Heavy Duty calls at his shop in Nashville, Tennessee. Call and decoy collecting has become a popular pastime among waterfowlers across the continent. Photo by Chris Dorsey.

A directory of modern duck calls:

1–HS Single Reed Mallard (plastic)
2–HS Single Reed Mallard (wooden)
3–Big River Mallard Custom Hook
4–Carlson Volochoke (plastic)
5–Carlson Custom (wooden)
6–Carlson Custom (wooden)
7–Olt DR-115 Double Reed (wooden)
8–Olt D-2 Regular (plastic)
9–Olt DD-120
10–Olt W-12 Pintail-Wigeon (plastic)
11–Olt mark V Mallard
12–Olt 66 Mallard (wooden)
13–Mallardtone M-5 (wooden)
14–Mallardtone TR-78 Double Reed (wooden)
15–Lohman 400 Pro Model (wooden)

16–Lohman Model 1000 (plastic)
17–Dixie Mallard Custom (wooden)
18–Knight & Hale Deluxe Mallard (wooden)
19–Faulk's WA-33 Deluxe Mallard
20–Woods Arkansas Style Mallard (wooden)
21–Catahoula Mallard Master (wooden)
22–Catahoula Mallard Master II (wooden)
23–Haydel's Double Reed Mallard (plastic)
24–Haydel's Double Reed Variable Tone Mallard (plastic)
25–Haydel's WM-91 Mallard (wooden)
26–Haydel's MP-90 Magnum Pintail Whistle
27–Rich-n-Tone Arkansas Mallard Double Reed (plastic)
28–Rich-n-Tone II Arkansas Mallard (plastic)
29–Sure-Shot Mallard 650 (plastic)
30–Sure-Shot Wood Duck (plastic)

A directory of modern goose calls:

1–Big River Long Honker (wooden)
2–Carlson Handcrafted Canada or Snow/Blue (wooden)
3–Olt Canada Honker (plastic)
4–Olt 800 Canada (wooden)
5–Olt 77 Canada (wooden)
6–Olt Regular Canada (plastic)
7–Mallardtone M-5 Canada
8–Lohman 5000 World Class Canada Flute (plastic)
9–Lohman 5500 Pro-Guide Canada Flute (plastic)
10–Knight & Hale Double Cluck Plus Canada (plastic)
11–Knight & Hale Magnum Clucker
12–Faulk's H-100 Canada Honker (wooden)
13–Faulk's Speckled Belly (wooden)
14–Woods Gander Land'r Flute (wooden)
15–Haydel's GF 88 Goose Flute (plastic)
16–Haydel's VTS 90 Variable Tone Snow (plastic)
17–Haydel's H-81 Canada Honker
18–Haydel's WF-91 Canada Flute
19–Haydel's CS-92 Cut Down Speck (plastic)
20–Sure-Shot 1150 Specklebelly

CALLING CONTESTS

Most competition callers acknowledge that there is a significant difference between calling ducks and performing on stage for judges. I have hunted with several successful competition callers, however, who were also skilled duck callers. Despite what some hunters might contend, it is possible to do both well.

For those who aspire to excel in competition calling, the name Stuttgart, Arkansas, has special meaning; it is home to the World Championship Duck Calling Contest, part of the annual Wings Over the Prairie Festival. This is the World Cup, Super Bowl, and Masters of

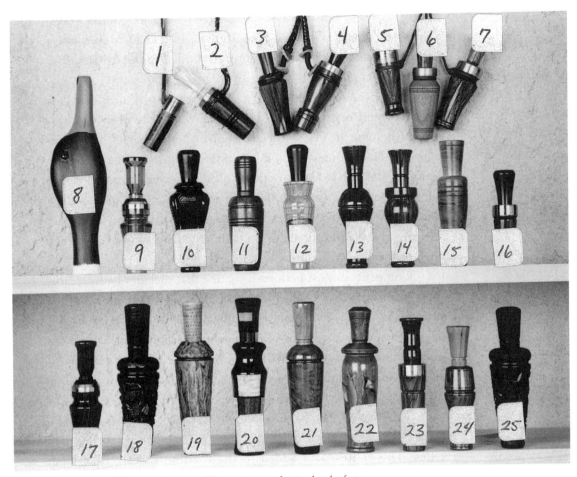

A selection of custom duck calls from across the country. They are, in essence, functional works of art.

1—Howard Harlan's Heavy Duty cocobola shotgun shell pintail/wigeon whistle

2—Gander Commander cocobola with acrylic insert

3—Howard Harlan's Heavy Duty cocobola duck call

4—Tom Cox's The Competition Calls cocobola call with brass band

5—Dick Burge call with walnut

6—Sam Barker call with walnut barrel and cedar insert

7—Dick Burge zebrawood with brass band

8—Jimmy Cerrata's The Duckhead

9—Grover Knoll's Cache River Duckall acrylic

10—Barry McFarland's Reel McDuck with ebony

11—Coats Call with walnut

12—Art Beauchamp Competition Call

13—Tom Weigel's Red River Duck Call with cocobola

14—Red River Duck Call with cocobola

15—John Gemmell Custom Call with French walnut

16—Mike Weller's Suzie Coaxer with cocobola

17—Grover Knoll's Cache River Duckall in cocobola

18—Kent Freeman's Ebony Duck Call

19—Bryan Schultz's call with walnut

20—Mike Fixter's Custom Call with ebony

21—Mike Fixter's Custom Call with walnut

22—Tom Condo's call with mahogany

23—Mike Weller's Red Leg Magnum with cocobola

24—Mike Fixter's Arkansas Style Call with walnut barrel and osage stopper

25—Kent Freeman's Ebony Goose Call

calling contests. The event began in 1936 when three Stuttgart residents—Dr. H. V. Glenn, Verne Tindall, and Thad McCollum—suggested that a duck-calling contest be added to the existing Rice Carnival.

While interest in the Rice Carnival eventually dwindled, the calling contest began to grow. Thomas E. Walsh, of Greenville, Mississippi, became the first world champion on November 24, 1936, winning a $6.60 hunting coat by distinguishing himself as the best caller among a field of seventeen entries. Today, several hundred callers annually vie for nearly $15,000 in cash and prizes and often receive offers to appear in advertisements and at sport shows. Many winners of the event have also capitalized on their newfound fame by launching their own call-manufacturing businesses.

Competitors must perform a routine that includes hail, feeding, mating, and comeback calls. Judges are typically experienced callers, many of whom have won multiple calling contests. World champions are automatically eligible to compete in the Champion of Champions competition, which began in 1955 and is held every five years. Winning this elite competition is the most prestigious of all duck-calling awards.

The World Championship Goose Calling Contest didn't begin until 1976, when Tim Covey won the first of his three consecutive titles. The contest was added to the existing Easton, Maryland, Waterfowl Festival, an annual event launched in 1971. Easton has long proclaimed itself the Goose Capital of the World, and goose-hunting traditions there run as deep as the currents in Chesapeake Bay.

The Mason-Dixon Regional Duck Calling Contest—a qualifier for the World Championship Duck Calling Contest—is held in conjunction with the annual goose-calling competition. Competitors in the goose contest must blow several calls—a rendition they would use to call a distant flock of geese to the blind. More than one thousand spectators regularly attend the event, and judges choose a winner from among hundreds of entries.

Hundreds of spectators gather to watch and listen to contestants at the 1994 World's Championship Duck Calling Contest held in Stuttgart, Arkansas. Call maker Buck Gardner went on to win the coveted title. Photo by Scott Liles.

World Champion Duck Callers

1936	Thomas E. Walsh, Greenville, Mississippi
1937	Harry R. Wieman, Stuttgart, Arkansas
1938	Harry R. Wieman, Stuttgart, Arkansas
1939	Kenneth McCollum, Stuttgart, Arkansas
1940	W. H. Claypool, Memphis, Tennessee
1941	M. T. McCollum, Stuttgart, Arkansas
1942	Herman Callouet, Greenville, Mississippi
1943	Clyde Hancock, Stuttgart, Arkansas
1944	Howard T. Conrey, Stuttgart, Arkansas
1945	D. M. "Chick" Major, Stuttgart, Arkansas
1946	Louis "Red" Wilhelm, Stuttgart, Arkansas
1947	J. E. "Jake" Gartner, Stuttgart, Arkansas
1948	J. E. "Jake" Gartner, Stuttgart, Arkansas
1949	J. E. "Jake" Gartner, Stuttgart, Arkansas
1950	Herb Parsons, Somerville, Tennessee
1951	Herb Parsons, Somerville, Tennessee
1952	W. C. Cowaan, Memphis, Tennessee
1953	Fred Parnell, Baton Rouge, Louisiana
1954	Art Beauchamp, Flint, Michigan
1955	Pat Stephens, Stuttgart, Arkansas
1956	Pat Stephens, Stuttgart, Arkansas
1957	W. C. Cross, Greenwood, Mississippi
1958	W. C. Cross, Greenwood, Mississippi
1959	James Fernandez, Port Arthur, Texas
1960	Ed Landreth, Joplin, Missouri
1961	Pete Claett, Kansas City, Missouri
1962	Charles Stepan, Port Arthur, Texas
1963	Mel DeLang, Burlington, Iowa
1964	Mick Lacy, Knoxville, Illinois
1965	John Liston, Knoxville, Illinois
1966	John Liston, Knoxville, Illinois
1967	Fred Harvey, Galesburg, Illinois
1968	Edward L. Holt, North Little Rock, Arkansas
1969	Edward L. Holt, North Little Rock, Arkansas
1970	Edward L. Holt, North Little Rock, Arkansas

1971   Larry Largent, Shelton, Nebraska

1972   Harry Richenback, Stuttgart, Arkansas

1973   Mike McLemore, Hendersonville, Tennessee

1974   Mike McLemore, Hendersonville, Tennessee

1975   Mike Starks, Little Rock, Arkansas

1976   Trey Crawford, North Little Rock, Arkansas

1977   Mike McLemore, Hallsville, Texas

1978   Richard Schultz, Cedar Rapids, Iowa

1979   Vernard Solomon, Marshall, Texas

1980   Dan Sprague, Buffalo, Iowa

1981   David Starks, Stuttgart, Arkansas

1982   Sam Hoeper, Grandview, Missouri

1983   Don Ansley, Nashville, Tennessee

1984   David Starks, Stuttgart, Arkansas

1985   Mike Keller, Kansas City, Missouri

1986   Trey Crawford, Mayflower, Arkansas

1987   David Javne, Clovis, California

1988   Johnny Mahfouz, Stuttgart, Arkansas

1989   Barnie Calef, Cedar Rapids, Iowa

1990   Roy Rhodes, Germantown, Tennessee

1991   Tim Gesch, Woodruff, Wisconsin

1992   Blake Haynes, Pine Bluff, Arkansas

1993   Trey Crawford, North Little Rock, Arkansas

1994   Buck Gardner, Germantown, Tennessee

Champion of Champions Duck Callers

1955   Art Beauchamp, Flint, Michigan

1960   Pat Stephens, Stuttgart, Arkansas

1965   John Liston, Knoxville, Illinois

1970   Edward L. Holt, North Little Rock, Arkansas

1975   Harry Richenback, Stuttgart, Arkansas

1980   Mike McLemore, Hendersonville, Tennessee

1985   David Starks, Stuttgart, Arkansas

1990   Johnny Mahfouz, Stuttgart, Arkansas

World Champion Goose Callers

1976   Tim Covey, Easton, Maryland
1977   Tim Covey, Easton, Maryland
1978   Tim Covey, Easton, Maryland
1979   Harold Knight, Cadiz, Kentucky
1980   Pete Rossing, Stevensville, Maryland
1981   Joe Bacon, Queenstown, Maryland
1982   David Coleman, Chestertown, Maryland
1983   William Privott, Currituck, North Carolina
1984   William Privott, Currituck, North Carolina
1985   Sean Mann, Easton, Maryland
1986   Sean Mann, Easton, Maryland
1987   Keith McGowan, Middletown, Delaware
1988   Tim Grounds, Johnson City, Illinois
1989   Keith McGowan, Middletown, Delaware
1990   Keith McGowan, Middletown, Delaware
1991   Allen McCree, Cartersville, Illinois
1992   Tim Grounds, Johnson City, Illinois
1993   Allen McCree, Cartersville, Illinois
1994   Tim Grounds, Johnson City, Illinois

VII

_P_resenting Decoys

Wooden decoys that once rode the waves of fabled wildfowling waters during the golden era now float on the calm surfaces of coffee tables and bookshelves, luring folk art collectors rather than ducks. In virtually every corner of America, decoy makers carved blocks with their own regional identity. As though looking for pieces of a great puzzle, collectors search for missing examples by noted carvers from across the country, preserving the traditions and memories of that lost time for a new generation of waterfowlers.

Waterfowl decoys spring from an ancient family tree with many branches. The two-thousand-year-old decoys discovered in Nevada's Lovelock Cave—the oldest existing examples—were fashioned of reeds in a manner typical of basket weaving of the period. The Tule Indian hunters lay in wait under water, breathing through hollow reed stems. When ducks were lured into range, they were netted, speared, or plucked from the water.

While bound reeds, stuffed skins, piled stones, and even clumps of kelp along tidal flats have all been used to lure waterfowl to stealthy hunters, the era of the modern decoy in America began with the golden age of waterfowling, a period that roughly encompassed the second half of the nineteenth century. While we disdain the wanton

Illustration from Gunner's Dawn, _1937._

Eastern Shore gunners set driver rigs using V-boards. Photo circa 1920. From the Joe Mitchell collection, courtesy of the Havre de Grace Decoy Museum.

slaughter of the market gunners, the decoys they created became the forerunners of the modern synthetic blocks we use today.

The early decoys were often crude facsimiles, hewn roughly from local stands of cedar. With time, the market hunters increasingly improved their proficiency at killing ducks and at making lifelike decoys. While market gunners used large spreads of wooden decoys, sport hunters employed live ducks and geese. Living decoys could also call birds to the gun—a practice so effective it was banned nationwide in 1935.

A few dedicated waterfowlers who adhere to the traditionalist's approach still carve their own decoys, yet few would argue that, in

Carver Bob McGaw adds the final coats of paint to one of his famous decoys. The Maryland native carved most of his decoys between 1920 and 1940. From the R. Madison Mitchell collection, courtesy of the Havre de Grace Decoy Museum.

practical terms, modern decoys are a radical improvement over the old wooden blocks. For the many waterfowlers who believe it is impossible for a decoy spread to be too large, the innovative new lightweight, stackable, and compactible designs allow a single hunter to carry and deploy dozens of decoys with the same effort it once took to rig a handful of the hefty blocks of yesteryear.

But decoys alone cannot always be counted on to pull birds within range. Where you hunt is at least as critical as how you hunt, for if the birds don't find the area surrounding your decoys inviting, they will fly on until they find another flock in a more enticing locale. This is where scouting is critical—whether hunting ducks or geese. Veteran hunters pay close attention to flight patterns throughout the day, noting when birds frequent favorite waters or fields.

Bob McGaw's decoys are individually tested in a tub to make sure they are seaworthy before being deployed by waterfowlers. From the Joe Mitchell collection, courtesy of the Havre de Grace Decoy Museum.

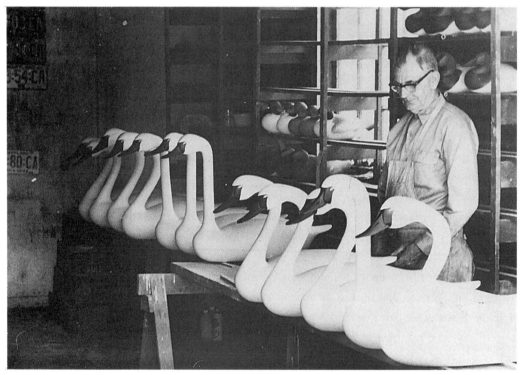

Madison Mitchell of Havre de Grace poses with a collection of his swan decoys. Mitchell was widely known as one of the finest decoy carvers on Chesapeake Bay. From the George Hipkins collection, courtesy of the Havre de Grace Decoy Museum.

As you study the movement of birds in your area, you'll begin to recognize identifiable patterns. This is all part of becoming a successful waterfowler, for even the best calling and decoy placements cannot compensate for a lack of scouting. Here is some advice on placing your decoys once you have found several areas to hunt.

DUCKING THE ISSUE

Just as ducks develop identifiable behavioral patterns, so too do duck hunters. It doesn't take birds long to associate shotgun fire with calls and decoys; by repeatedly using the same spreads and calls, hunters often wind up teaching ducks to avoid a given area. Savvy hunters alternate their call-decoy delivery.

You will want to vary the size of your spread according to the size of the water and the species of ducks you are most likely to encounter. When hunting pressure is intense, ducks often search for small, secluded wetlands or pockets of hidden, flooded timber where they can escape the barrage. Small spreads can be highly inviting under these circumstances; ducks might be wary of an overabundance of decoys crammed into a tiny waterhole. Despite what some believe, it is possible to over-decoy just as it is possible to over-call.

Rather than always using a large spread, try adding movement to a smaller decoy rig. One time-honored method involves placing a brick with a hole in it under your decoys. Tie a string to the decoy and run it through the hole in the brick, then back to your blind. The brick and string will keep the decoy in place, and with a few short jerks on the string the decoy will bob about like a live bird. This can be especially seductive to ducks on calm days, when decoys typically look as flaccid as the water upon which they are floating. The added movement might be the edge you need to convince skeptical birds to approach. To make your spread even more convincing, rig several decoys this way and your marionette routine will begin to show results in your daily bag. Black or dark-colored string is the best, for the birds might detect light-colored twine.

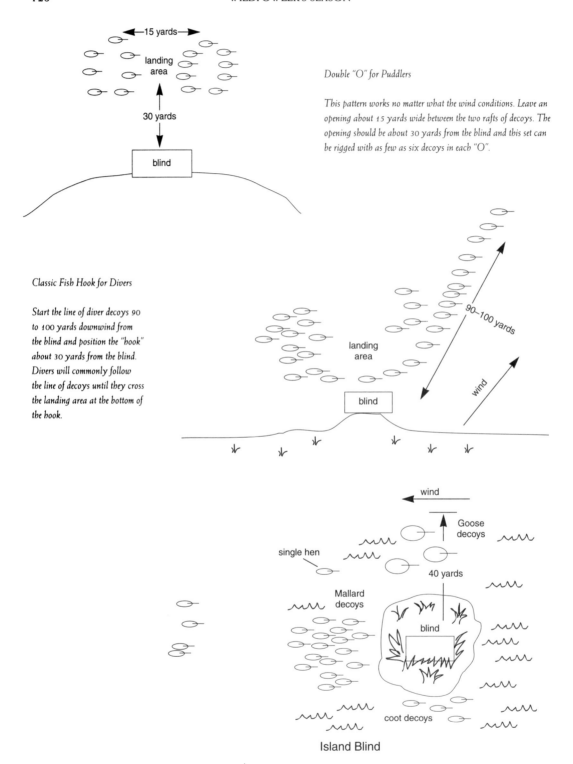

Double "O" for Puddlers

This pattern works no matter what the wind conditions. Leave an opening about 15 yards wide between the two rafts of decoys. The opening should be about 30 yards from the blind and this set can be rigged with as few as six decoys in each "O".

Classic Fish Hook for Divers

Start the line of diver decoys 90 to 100 yards downwind from the blind and position the "hook" about 30 yards from the blind. Divers will commonly follow the line of decoys until they cross the landing area at the bottom of the hook.

15 yards

landing area

30 yards

blind

landing area

90–100 yards

wind

blind

wind

Goose decoys

single hen

40 yards

Mallard decoys

blind

coot decoys

Island Blind

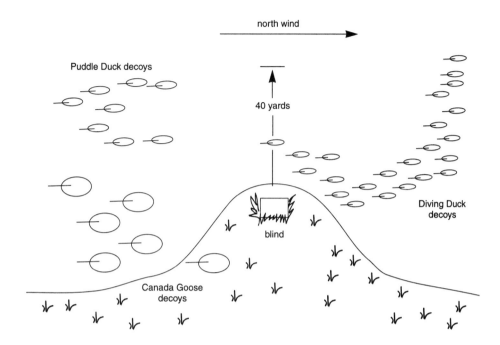

Point Blind

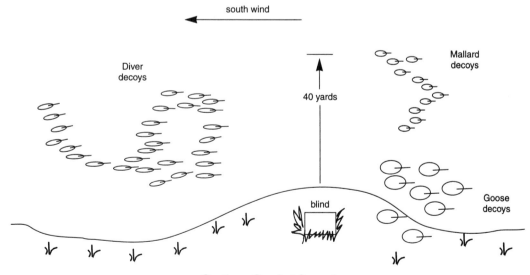

Southern Comfort Spread

Check out the prices in 1939. These ads appeared in Sports Afield *and give an early indication of the innovative nature of wildfowlers.*

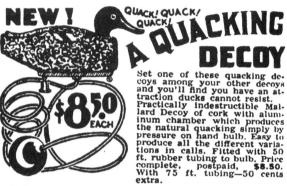

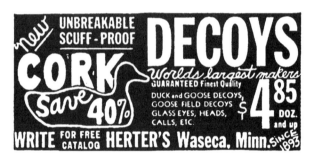

Another common trick that can help turn wary birds your way when hunting in flooded timber is to perform the duck stroke, splashing your feet in the water as birds make their initial pass over the decoys. Ducks are apt to notice the ripples—the same waves they associate with feeding ducks. Some hunters also like to stir up the marsh or woodland bottom with their feet as they walk through the water placing decoys. The floating debris imitates water where a flock of ducks is busily feeding and churning up the bottom.

Many hunters have added "flying" decoys to their spreads to heighten the element of realism. These decoys, designed to imitate ducks or geese in flight, give spreads an accentuated, three-dimensional appearance. Some hunters would not be without such decoys, others remain skeptical. As with any waterfowling technique, it's best to test the method yourself under conditions you commonly experience.

Winged decoys are designed to help further the illusion of movement and add realism to decoy spreads. Photo by Chris Dorsey.

When thinking about your decoy presentation, remember that how you set a rig can be as important as how many decoys you deploy. Too often, waterfowlers neglect the subtle details. For instance, cluttering the water in front of your blind with a haphazard arrangement of decoys may keep birds away from your gun instead of bringing them in. A well-seasoned Mississippi River guide once told me to think of decoys as airport landing lights for ducks; they should direct birds to a certain spot near the blind—preferably to a location that will take

Be careful to keep decoy lines untangled, otherwise you may wind up with a mess of knotted chords. Several products to help you do just that are now available through many specialty catalogs. Photo by Chris Dorsey.

them within easy shotgun range. That, simplified, is the essence of decoying ducks.

Remember also that each species of duck reacts differently to decoy spreads, depending on how they feed. Puddle ducks do not commonly feed in a long line on the water, diving ducks do. Deploy your decoy spread accordingly and your retriever will be more likely to find work.

We know that birds can perceive color, and most experienced waterfowlers believe that puddle ducks are much more likely to be fooled by decoys whose colors closely mimic those of real birds. Diving ducks, on the other hand, routinely decoy to black jugs tied to a long rope. Since any duck must be able to see your blocks before it will approach them, there is much debate over whether clear dawns or foggy mornings provide the best conditions for duck hunting. Wildlife artists are fond of portraying waterfowling scenes fit for a polar bear—snow and rain blowing horizontally against a backdrop of rough seas. Most decoy manufacturers I've talked with, however, agree that well-lit days are the best times to decoy ducks. Of course, if the birds can see the decoys better, they can also spot movement in a nearby blind more easily. Properly placed decoys help draw attention away from movements in the blind, becoming both attractions and distractions.

Finally, leaving decoys in the same position for the entire season will likely mean increasingly less shooting; ducks soon learn to tell a static spread from live ducks. In many states it's illegal to leave decoys unattended in the water, but if for no other reason, decoys should be picked up to keep from educating birds.

GOOSE FOOLERY

The remarkable resurgence of geese across North America has created unprecedented hunting opportunities in areas where the birds were never before seen. Geese have found crop residue from the continent's extensive cereal grain production to their liking, converting the high-calorie foods into added weight as the birds enter the breeding season.

Nature photographer Lon Lauber takes a break from work to try his hand at bowhunting for Canada geese near Minnesota's Lac Qui Parle goose refuge. The decoy spread consisted of Real Geese silhouettes. Photo by Chris Dorsey.

Unlike many duck species, which often nest in agricultural regions, geese nest farther north, away from areas prone to wetland drainage and development. This allows goose populations to thrive even when duck numbers dwindle during the droughts that afflict the Prairie Pothole Country of the Great Plains—a region known as North America's Duck Factory.

Increases in goose numbers have interested a whole new generation of wildfowlers in goose decoys. Consequently, several manufacturers have introduced new assortments that are both more lifelike and considerably lighter and easier to carry than decoys used by their early ancestors. This has made it far easier to deploy large numbers of de-

Scouting a day earlier revealed that this field was serving as a diner for area geese. Canadas faithfully return to a field in which they fed the day before, and if they don't receive heavy hunting pressure while using such a field, they will often return until all the spilled grain is gone. Here, Wisconsin hunters position a mixture of Bigfoot and shell decoys to attract birds to waiting gunners. Photo by Chris Dorsey.

coys in a short amount of time—an important consideration for waterfowlers who want to hunt over the largest possible decoy spreads.

When surveying the ever-growing field of goose decoys, it's important to understand that what might look good to a hunter might not look so good to a goose. Manufacturers know that geese don't buy decoys, hunters do. Conversely, what may look ridiculous to hunters might, in fact, prove an effective goose attractant. For instance, outsized decoys, many times the size of normal geese, often prove more effective than standard-size decoys.

Geese lured by gigantic decoys are responding to what animal behavioralists call supernormal stimuli. In one study, scientists placed a wooden egg, identical in shape and color to a typical herring gull egg but 20 times normal size, next to a normal-size egg in front of a nesting herring gull. The gull repeatedly tried to incubate the outsized egg, awkwardly falling off in the process. So strong was its urge to incubate

Herter's Webfoot decoy is a full-body representation of a goose. While full-body decoys might appear the most lifelike of all decoy configurations—save for the "stuffers" prepared by taxidermists on the Eastern Shore—they are often bulky and difficult to deploy in large numbers. Some hunters, then, mix silhouette decoys with full-body dupes to expand the size of a spread.

the huge egg that it abandoned its own egg. Scientists believe that form and size are the two key elements to attracting birds—important points when shopping for goose decoys.

Other than this notion of supernormal stimuli, there is little scientific evidence to tell us how geese react as they fly over a flock of decoys. Consequently, there is much speculation about what types of decoys and presentations work best. One of the most basic guidelines to follow is to look for forms with paint that won't flake off, and that have been treated to prevent ultraviolet light damage.

If you are hunting geese over water, note the movement of floating geese. In waves, geese tip from front to back, so you'll want to buy decoys that do the same, avoiding those that roll from side to side. Success in waterfowling is often found in attending to these seemingly minor details.

As with duck decoys, adding movement to a goose spread can be effective in conning gun-shy geese. Hunters have long known that flagging can be a superb way to capture the attention of a distant flock of passing geese. The birds are not drawn by a waving flag per se, they are catching a glimpse of movement in the flock—not unlike a bird flapping its wings. Flagging has been further refined to include a wide selection of "flying" decoys, which are fitted with attachments designed to resemble wings. Hunters can even flap the wings of some models by pulling on a cord. Other decoys have movable heads and necks, again a recognition of the importance of movement in decoys.

The size of a decoy spread is a primary consideration and a source of great debate among goose hunters. Most agree that the larger the spread, the greater a hunter's chance of taking geese. Others contend that it's better to use a small spread and continually move the decoys to new hunting areas. If you are hunting in a permanent blind near a refuge, you won't have the option of relocating your decoys, but you can alternate the size of your spread and its position. Whatever type of spread you prefer, it's wise to gather your decoys when you fin-

Waterfowl seem to be growing wiser as hunters seemingly do their best to educate birds. "Flying" decoys like these offered by Cabela's are an attempt to add realism to otherwise static decoy spreads. Photo by Chris Dorsey.

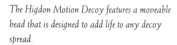

The Higdon Motion Decoy features a moveable head that is designed to add life to any decoy spread.

Despite using enormous spreads of rags and wind socks, snow geese can be difficult to decoy. This crescent-shaped pattern was used to little effect on the wheat fields of North Dakota. Photo by Chris Dorsey.

ish shooting; the longer geese become accustomed to the blocks, the less likely they are to visit them. Moreover, leaving decoys out overnight invites theft, and if frost forms on the stool, geese often avoid them; real geese don't reflect light like iced decoys.

Many guides like to mix silhouette and full-body decoys to give a spread the varied look of a flock. It is widely accepted that a spread's overall look is far more important than the appearance of an individual decoy—though the two are certainly related—for geese are not looking at a single decoy as much as they are the appearance of the whole flock. When geese fly past silhouette decoys, the two-dimensional forms appear to move, looking as though they are geese turning away, depending on the angle from which they are viewed. Most hunters avoid combining large- and small-shell decoys, for if they appear incongruous to us, think how they must appear to geese.

Depending on how many decoys you feel you will need to lure geese, you will have to determine which kind of stool you can readily deploy. From the stubble fields of North Dakota to the rice prairies of southern Texas, rags have traditionally been used to decoy snow geese. It's easy to cover the ground with white rags in a fraction of the time it takes to deploy full-body or shell decoys. The question, though, is whether more rags are better at decoying geese than are fewer numbers of full-body or shell decoys. The rags are certainly cheaper, but are they lifelike enough to fool sophisticated geese that have been hunted since leaving their breeding grounds in northern Canada? Rags, too, often blow across fields in the wind and may snap in a heavy breeze, spooking geese as the birds approach within earshot.

I remember this question being on the minds of several south-Texas goose guides one year when an especially cold and wet spring in the subarctic resulted in an unusually poor goose hatch. The birds migrating south over the hunting fields were predominantly two or more years old, veteran geese that had seen their share of rag spreads. Log entries at goose clubs across Texas indicated it was one of the worst harvest years on record, though there were plenty of geese around. Toward the end of the frustrating season, some guides began to abandon their rag spreads in favor of full-body, silhouette, or shell decoys. For

Decoy designer Tom Farmer introduced his line of Farm Form Waddler decoys to improve on the rags so often used in his native Texas. These dupes get their name because they fidget in the wind, adding the important element of movement to the spread.

many, the results were astounding. While yearling birds seem perfectly willing to decoy to rags, older birds tend to flare from them before approaching within shotgun range.

For hunters who want a large spread without using rags, stackable decoys are available that can be deployed in almost the same amount of time it takes to throw rags on the ground. Some of these models not only give a full-body look, but also mount on stakes that allow the decoys to fidget with the wind, adding movement to the stool. Again, before purchasing your goose decoys consider these questions:

- How large a spread do I want?
- How long does it take to deploy prospective decoys?
- How lifelike do the birds appear?
- Do the decoys have inherent movement?
- Can I achieve the flock effect using these decoys?
- How much do the decoys cost versus how long they can be expected to last?

Being able to quickly deploy decoy spreads is important to many hunters. Here, Feather Flex's Dave Berkley demonstrates such a virtue in his goose decoys. Photo by Chris Dorsey.

While skillful calling may overcome some inadequacies in decoy presentation, nothing beats a good decoy spread in a prime location— a freshly picked cornfield or newly cut wheatfield. Goose hunters know that geese—especially Canadas—usually return in the morning to where they were feeding the previous night. Hunters who want good shooting in the morning will need to spend time scouting the previous evening. Though you cannot control the birds, your calling, decoys, and location can greatly influence their movement. If there is an art to goose hunting, it is in blending all three of these components effectively.

VIII

*W*by a Retriever?

Hunting waterfowl without a retriever is, for many hunters, a drama without the supporting cast, a canoe without a paddle, ice and tonic without the gin. Plenty of statistics tell us that hunters accompanied by trained retrievers are more likely to bring home game, and there is certainly much to be said for minimizing lost birds, but perhaps we prefer hunting with retrievers as much for their companionship as for their practical usefulness.

When there is no one else to brave the cold north wind and snow the last weekend of the season, there is always your retriever, as eager as he was his first season. He needs no convincing, does not particularly care if the ducks are flying in earnest, and will not complain if there is no work—save for a few whines when gunshots bring no results. Of all the hunting breeds, retrievers are the easiest to talk to, for they are the best listeners. Even if they don't understand what you're saying, they often give the impression they do—a skill we come to cherish in any good friend. Retrievers are effective alibis, too, for when you return home three hours late they'll accept the blame without holding a grudge. Ultimately, your retriever is the one entity on the planet that shares your passion for the marsh, your eagerness to witness the dawn flights, and your reverence for the sport and the glory that goes with it.

Illustration from Shooting on Upland, Marsh, and Stream, *1890.*

Training your own retriever is about becoming a complete waterfowler. Each element of the sport—whether calling, decoy placement,
shooting, boating, blind construction, or retriever training—adds its
own challenges and virtues. As you gain proficiency in each of these

Before buying a retriever, be sure you are ready for the commitment of time, affection, and money that goes along with dog ownership. Photo by Chuck Petrie.

areas, you heighten your overall enjoyment of the sport. The many nuances of waterfowling mean you never truly master it so much as it simply seduces you. The engaging nature of a good retriever is what led many of us to fall for it in the first place, leading us down the path of the waterfowler's life—a journey marked by memories and friendships to last a lifetime.

ABOUT RETRIEVERS

Exactly when man first employed a dog to retrieve game is a matter of speculation, but we do know that dogs with a propensity to retrieve existed long before there was a class of dogs known as retrievers. Most modern retrievers are descendants of the original water spaniels; the oldest English retriever that still exists as an identifiable breed is the curly-coated retriever.

It's hard not to admire a retriever that will brave frigid temperatures and rough water so that its master might have a duck dinner.
Photo by Chris Dorsey.

While most retrievers are especially well adapted for water work, many also excel in the uplands, a fact to which countless pheasants, grouse, and quail can personally attest. Retrievers are also known for their pleasant nature, which accounts for their popularity with the nonhunting public. Of the 1.4 million dogs registered with the American Kennel Club in 1993, for instance, Labradors were number one—124,899 of them—testimony to the success and versatility of the breed.

If you're thinking about purchasing a retriever, remember that many dogs are bred as pets, their only work perhaps coming in the show ring. When selecting a dog, examine its registration papers carefully for evidence of hunting ancestry. Look for the initials FC and AFC, which mean Field trial Champion and Amateur Field trial Champion in a pup's pedigree. This will indicate a history of field work. Dogs with "Ch" appearing in several places on their pedigrees have been shown more often than hunted.

Even better indicators of a pup's future success are its parents. Ask to see both the sire and the bitch if possible, and don't be shy about asking questions like: Have both dogs been hunted? Were their par-

In flooded bottomlands, many hunters attach stands to trees to give their retrievers a place to stand without being submerged in water for long periods of time. Photo by Chris Dorsey.

ents hunted? Any history of dysplasia or any other hereditary health problems? You will also get an idea of the pup's probable size at maturity by seeing its parents. Make sure a pup has received all necessary shots before purchasing it. Many breeders also have a dog's dewclaws removed shortly after whelping, saving potential problems later, as these claws serve no purpose and are prone to snagging and ripping on brush. Each pup should also have an individual health card signed by a veterinarian—this is your dog's bill of health.

Don't be bashful about asking to see the parents hunt. If possible, have the sire perform some rudimentary retrieves and note the proficiency with which the dog performs them. Though the dam's recent pregnancy may mean she is in no condition to work, you might inquire if the owner has photos of her on past hunts or, better yet, a video of the dog performing in the field.

Handle the parents, petting them and noting their dispositions. You will increase your chances of getting a dog you will be happy with by carefully checking its background. One way to avoid possible problems is to get a pup from a dog with which you have hunted on several occasions. Pups are often purchased by a breeder's friends who have been impressed by a dog's hunting ability; nothing sells pups faster than parents with a reputation of being fine hunters. Truly promising litters are often spoken for far in advance of actual whelping, so be cautious about buying a pup from a person who has had difficulty selling his or her pups. Several breeds of retrievers are prone to having large litters, however, and even good dogs sometimes are difficult to move when there are, say, fifteen pups in a litter. Don't automatically rule out such dogs; just plan on conducting a systematic background check of any prospect.

Many perfectly sound hunting dogs have been bought via newspaper ads, if such ads were treated merely as leads on which to follow up with more questioning. Purchasing a pup from a pet shop is a far greater risk, for some shops are merely retail outlets for puppy mills, high-volume operations with little regard for quality breeding regimens. If it's hunting stock you're after, the best advice is to simply avoid such places altogether.

A retriever that will stay put until given a command to fetch is an asset to any waterfowler. An unruly dog, on the other hand, can be at worst a danger and at best a nuisance. Photo by Chris Dorsey.

You'll want to pick the retrieving breed best suited to your style of hunting. If you are primarily a goose hunter, you'll need a dog large and strong enough to manage hefty geese—though I've seen plenty of small dogs capable of toting even large honkers. If you often hunt in icy water, you'll want a breed equipped to cope with such conditions. If you spend much time hunting the uplands, some retrievers are better at it than others. Here, then, is a profile of the retrieving breeds—their ancestry, strengths, and weaknesses.

LABRADOR RETRIEVER

Few breeds anywhere have enjoyed the success of the Labrador retriever, a dog whose roots are planted in England rather than Labrador, as its name implies. Its amenable nature and intelligence help make it

On Kodiak Island, Alaska, retrievers like this Lab are more than water dogs—they also help keep watch for roaming bears. Photo by Chris Dorsey.

far and away the most popular retrieving breed in North America. The late Richard Wolters, one of America's authorities on the Labrador, once described the breed this way: "The Labrador is the king of retrievers. . . . He is intelligent but not cunning; he's lovable but not soft. The Labrador retriever is loyal but not a one-man dog. He's gentle but not a dog to be backed against the wall. He's a romping fun fellow but won his crown as an honest worker."

It is believed that Labs stem from a French dog called the St. Hubert's hound, a breed brought to England in the sixteenth century. Modern Labs originated on the British Isles in the 1800s, from dogs bred primarily to satisfy the needs of gamekeepers charged with running the driven shoots then gaining widespread popularity among the English aristocracy. The advent of the breech-loading shotgun in the mid-nineteenth century meant that often grotesque numbers of birds were shot, and the easily trained Labs were in great demand for the rigors of high-volume retrieving.

A few wealthy Americans who had traveled to the United Kingdom sampled the British driven shooting and imported the practice to America—bringing the Labrador retriever with them. The Labs did not gain widespread acceptance among American hunters until they began to dominate the field trial scene in the 1930s. Where once the Chessie and American water spaniel had been the favorite among trialers and gunners alike, the Lab's proficiency now proved superior. Waterfowlers took note and began to test the dogs under hunting conditions, and the breed quickly won favor among even ardent fans of other breeds.

There are an estimated 2 million hunting Labs in America today—a remarkable statistic considering that there are fewer than 1.5 million waterfowl hunters in the United States. The breed has grown enormously popular with nonhunters as well. Many Labs also excel in upland work for such species as pheasants and grouse. Their propensity to work close makes them an effective choice for a variety of upland duties and, when game is flushed, it is likely to be presented within shooting range.

Modern Labs vary widely in size. Many of the smaller, sleeker Labs often perform well for long periods in the uplands, while the larger, 70 pounds and up may find the daily rigors of pounding the fields difficult. Conversely, the smaller Labs may be too small to retrieve a giant Canada goose weighing more than 15 pounds.

For the first-time retriever owner with a mind to develop an effective hunting companion, the Lab is a good choice. Remember that color is not nearly as important as sound breeding, so it's wise to make your selection after a thorough background check of any prospective pup.

Breed Specifications: Average height from 20 to 23 inches; weight, 55 to 75 pounds. Builds range from short and stout to tall and lean, with a thick nose and pointed head. Eyes, chestnut or hazel, ears hang against the head, the neck is broad and powerful. The tail is long and sturdy at the base. The dense coat comes in black, yellow, or chocolate.

GOLDEN RETRIEVER

Many waterfowlers knew of the golden's versatility long ago, but when former President Gerald Ford kept one at the White House, the breed instantly reached celebrity status. The demand for goldens soon eclipsed the supply, and prices for the dogs began to climb. Nearly seventy thousand goldens were registered with the AKC in 1993, making them the second-most-popular retrieving breed behind Labradors, and fifth most popular of all breeds.

In addition to being playful family companions, goldens are perhaps the most adept upland hunters of the retrievers. They are fleet of foot and graceful when traversing cover, and most have the endurance for several consecutive days of demanding work in heavy cover. Sometimes goldens are criticized for lacking the Chesapeake's tolerance for cold water and icy conditions, but I've hunted with some that seem unaware of their supposed deficiencies. I met one while hunting sea ducks near Kodiak Island, Alaska, one cold December day. The dog's coat was so thick it more closely resembled a heavy-maned simba than it did a canine. It made several long retrieves in frigid waters where tidal currents made returning to shore an exasperating experience.

Sir Dudley Marjoribanks of Scotland developed the breed by crossing the now-extinct Tweed water spaniel with what was then called a wavy-coated (or flat-coated) retriever. The dogs from this and subsequent breedings were originally considered merely blond-color phases of the flat-coat, but by 1913, the golden retriever was recognized as a separate breed by the English Kennel Club. The American Kennel Club accepted the golden retriever as a distinct breed in 1932.

Though most goldens in America today are bred for the show ring, the breed continues to enjoy an avid following among waterfowlers—especially those who also want a dog for upland bird hunting. With the preponderance of American goldens having show backgrounds, it's especially important to examine carefully any prospective pup's pedigree and parents.

The golden's long coat may help insulate it during water retrieves, but it can also be a burr magnet in the uplands. Nonetheless, goldens are vigorous working dogs, among the easiest to train of all retrievers.

Breed Specifications: Average height from 21 to 24 inches; weight, 60 to 75 pounds. Has a large muzzle, dark eyes, a long tail, and a shiny, wavy coat with pronounced feathering along chest, tail, and back of legs. Coat ranges in color from cream to gold.

CHESAPEAKE BAY RETRIEVER

The Chessie is one of only four sporting breeds to be developed on the North American continent. There is some disagreement over the breed's origins. In 1807, George Law helped rescue the crew of a British vessel along with two St. John's dog pups. Law later wrote of the dogs' ability to retrieve waterfowl in the cold waters of the Chesapeake Bay. He also noted that one of the pups, a male with a dingy red coat, sported unusually light-colored eyes.

According to most experts, though, the Chessie is probably a genetic blend of several breeds, including pointers, setters, flat-coated retrievers, Irish water spaniels, and even black-and-tan hounds. Early names of the Chessie included the Gunpowder River dog, brown Winchester, otter dog, and Chesapeake Bay duck dog. Market gunners along the Atlantic tidewaters came to rely on the Chessie's ability to endure long periods in icy water. These dogs were often required to fetch a hundred ducks or more on a given day or night.

Actor Jameson Parker and his Chesapeake watch another flight of pintails descend over the blind they recently vacated. With three mallards and a pintail collected from the morning shoot, the birds in the marsh will have the afternoon to rest. Photo by Chris Dorsey.

The Chessie's detractors often call it mean and stubborn—one part wolf, one part mule. Fans defend the Chessie with remarkable vigor, however, contending that Chessies are courageous, tough, and ideally suited to cold-water work where most dogs fail. Indeed, no breed can negotiate cold water and ice better than the Chessie, and, in my experience, they can be quite gentle. As with any breed, mistreatment can create a disagreeable dog, a more likely cause of problems than the Chessie's innate disposition. I've also found their reputation for being aggressive is often exaggerated, though they do tend to be extremely loyal to their masters.

The breed's large size and toughness make it an exceptional goose retriever—both on land and on water. Their thick, wiry overcoat and woolly, insulating undercoat feel oily, which helps the breed shrug off cold and ice.

Breed Specifications: Average height from 21 to 26 inches; weight, 55 to 75 pounds. Has a wide head with stout muzzle and yellowish eyes; a deep chest, pendant ears, and thick fur, ranging in color from light red to dark chestnut to dead grass.

FLAT-COATED RETRIEVER

This breed was once a favorite among British gamekeepers who preferred a close-working retriever with an exceptional nose. Its origins date back to nineteenth-century England, where water spaniels, Irish setters, and Gordon setters were mixed with the St. John's dog (the breed from which both the Chesapeake and Labrador descended). The infusion of setter blood probably accounts for this breed's keen scenting abilities. S. E. Shirley, one of the early developers of the flat-coat, was a well-known breeder in England and founded the English Kennel Club in 1873. He reportedly bred several litters of flat-coats at his kennels before 1850. Many

The flat-coated retrievers are difficult to find. They are not only fine water dogs, but excel in upland work as well. Photo by Barbara D. Krieger.

experts also credit Dr. Bond Moore of Wolverhampton with having been largely responsible for the breed's creation.

The breed remains quite rare in the United States; in 1993, only 485 were registered with the AKC. Nevertheless, flat-coats are amiable and affectionate dogs that make superb personal hunting companions—particularly in the uplands, where their setterlike conformation seems especially well suited.

Breed Specifications: Average height from 22 to 23 inches; weight, 60 to 70 pounds. It has dark brown eyes, a deep chest, and a long tail. Coat is thick, fine textured, flat, and most often black or liver colored.

CURLY-COATED RETRIEVER

As the name implies, this dog's curly coat makes it resemble a poodle, and in fact it likely descends from a combination of poodle and St. John's dog. The tight curls on this breed's fur serve a utilitarian purpose, protecting it from ice and cold water. Like the Chesapeake, the curly-coated retriever is an exceptional cold-water retriever, and the curly fur doesn't collect burrs as readily as one might imagine at first glance.

Curly-coated retrievers make excellent pets and family dogs and are large and strong enough to handle even wounded geese. Though they are often slow to mature, they retain training lessons well, reducing the amount of retraining necessary to produce an effective hunter each season.

Breed Specifications: Average height from 25 to 27 inches; weight, 65 to 70 pounds. Dark eyes, large head, black nose, and pointed muzzle. Coat varies from liver to black.

IRISH WATER SPANIEL

This dog's unique appearance stems from an unlikely ancestral mixture of the St. John's dog, the curly-coated retriever, and the poodle. Its origins date back to the mid-1800s, when a hunter from Dublin, Justin M.

The curly-coated retriever likely gets its curly fur from the poodle, which was probably bred with the St. John's dog to create the curly-coated retriever. Photo by Janean Marti.

McCarthy, developed the breed from the northern Irish water spaniel and the southern Irish water spaniel. McCarthy's dog, Boatswain, is believed to be the "father" of this breed. By the mid-nineteenth century, Irish water spaniels were being used along the Mississippi River, in the Flyway of the Mallard. While these dogs enjoyed some popularity during the 1920s, they have since faded to near obscurity. Only 135 Irish water spaniels were registered with the AKC in 1993. While their coat is well suited to prolonged exposure to cold water, it attracts burrs and debris, making it difficult to maintain.

Breed Specifications: Average height from 20 to 23 inches; weight, 55 to 60 pounds. Has a large head, a long, square muzzle with short hair, and small, brown eyes. Its coat is thick with tight curls, oily, and long. Coat color is most often dark liver.

The Nova Scotia duck tolling retriever serves as both a decoy of sorts and as a retriever. The dogs lure swimming ducks within range of waiting hunters by simply playing along the shoreline in front of the gunners. Oddly enough, wildfowl are almost compelled to swim toward the dogs, satiating their curiosity about the dogs.
Photo by Jeff Howard.

NOVA SCOTIA DUCK TOLLING RETRIEVER

In the world of sporting dogs, this one is unique. The tolling retriever acts as both a decoy and a retriever. As hunters sit hidden in blinds along the edge of a lake, river, or bay, they allow their tolling dog to play nearby, running up and down the bank. Ducks, upon seeing this, begin swimming curiously toward the dog to get a closer look. Nineteenth-century author J. S. Skinner wrote that the practice of using a dog for tolling started in Maryland about 1800. Others claim that the tolling dog was developed in the Little River area near Yarmouth, Nova Scotia.

Henry Folkard, in his book, *The Wildfowler*, published in London in 1864, wrote that "tolling . . . is said to have been first introduced near Havre-de-Grace, in Maryland; and, according to traditional testimony, the art was accidentally discovered by a sportsman whilst patiently lying in ambush watching a paddling of wild ducks, which were a little beyond the range of his gun. Whilst in a state of doubt and anxiety as to whether they would approach near enough to be shot, he suddenly observed them raising their heads and swimming towards the shore apart from his ambuscade; and whilst wondering at the cause of so strange a proceeding, his attention was directed to a fox which was skipping about on the shore, and evidently enticing the ducks to approach."

There is evidence, however, that European hunters trained fox-colored dogs to toll ducks into awaiting nets before a tolling dog existed in North America. The dog derives its name from the word "tollen," a Middle-English term that means to lure or attract. French Acadians or Scots might have been the first to bring the breed to North America. The modern Nova Scotia Duck Tolling Retriever likely has a mixture of Chesapeake, spitz, collie, springer spaniel, and perhaps even beagle blood in it. The dog was recognized by the Canadian Kennel Club as a distinct breed in 1945, but the AKC has yet to do so.

Breed Specifications: Medium-size, muscular dog resembling a red fox. Has a thick coat from golden in color to nearly red. It sports a long, bushy tail often with a white tip. White markings are also common on the face and chest.

HUNTING TESTS FOR RETRIEVERS

Field trials for retrievers in America began in the 1930s, with Chesapeake Bay retrievers dominating the early events. The Labrador's arrival, however, brought that reign to an end. The level of training and breeding needed to develop a successful field trial retriever today far exceeds the requirements of the average hunter. If you watch a contemporary retriever trial, you might be intimidated by the degree of

National Bird Dog Museum

If you find yourself in the vicinity of Grand Junction, Tennessee, you'll want to visit the National Bird Dog Museum. While much of the museum is dedicated to famous pointing dog handlers and their dogs, it houses the Retriever Hall of Fame as well. Visitors get a close-up look at original portraits of some truly remarkable dogs, past champions that have reached legendary status among retriever followers. The museum was built by people who share a general affection for gun dogs, whether they are upland or water specialists. Through the thoughtful and tireless effort of volunteers across the country, this museum leaves a visitor with a sense of the rich history wingshooters share with their canine companions.

AKC HUNTING TEST FOR RETRIEVERS

Official Evaluation Form

Name of Dog_____

AKC Reg. No._____   TEST LEVEL (JR SR MH) Circle One

ABILITIES	1	2	3	4	5	6	7	Average
I. MARKING Memory								
II. STYLE								
III. NOSE								
IV. PERSEVERANCE Courage								
V. TRAINABILITY Steadiness, control, response and delivery								

Series #

NOTE: If, at any time during testing, a dog is graded zero (0) by two Judges for the same ability, the dog cannot receive a Qualifying score and the handler must be informed that the dog cannot receive a Qualifying score, even though the Judges may elect to continue to test the dog in further planned series.

©1985. THE AMERICAN KENNEL CLUB

TOTAL

DIVIDE TOTAL BY
5 FOR OVERALL AVERAGE

The back of this sheet should be used for diagramming each test in each series.

A look at the score sheet for AKC Hunting Tests gives you an idea of what judges are looking for in working retrievers.

control many of these trainers have over their dogs. These dogs are the high-performance race cars of the dog world, well-tuned and polished. Enjoy them for the quality animals they are, but do not hold yourself or your pup up to the standards of professionals and professionally trained dogs. Set attainable goals for each of you, and you'll find greater satisfaction with your dog. Three organizations that sponsor hunting retriever tests are:

American Kennel Club
51 Madison Ave.
New York, NY 10010

United Kennel Club
100 East Kilgore Rd.
Kalamazoo, MI 49001

North American Hunting
   Retriever Association
P.O. Box 1590
Stafford, VA 22555

Field tests, like the Ducks Unlimited Retriever Classic pictured here, allow hunters and trainers the chance to compare the abilities of competing dogs. Photo by Chris Dorsey.

IX

Dressing for Fowl Weather

Midwestern duck hunters who were in their favorite blinds on November 11, 1940, will never forget that day. The morning began with mild temperatures that climbed to nearly 60 degrees, and many hunters went to their blinds with nothing but light jackets. By late afternoon, temperatures had plummeted to 15 degrees and a bitter

Illustration from American Duck Shooting, *1901.*

northwest wind blew with gale strength. One gust of 80 miles per hour was recorded at the airport in Milwaukee, Wisconsin. On Lake Michigan, the steamer *William B. Davocks* broke in half, sending nearly 80 sailors to icy graves.

Hunters caught by the sudden ferocity of the storm could do little but surrender to the elements and hope. Newspaper accounts reported harrowing tales of stranded duck hunters surviving the storm by taking shelter under their boats and huddling next to their retrievers. One Wisconsin hunter described his experience this way: "It was like being on an ice cake in the middle of hell."

Some thirty-nine duck hunters perished in the Armistice Day storm. Author Wendell Smith wrote: "When there are promises of flying ducks and a dark cloud on the western horizon with snow in the forecast, there are hunters who reach into their memories, and they throw an extra jacket into the boat before leaving for the blind."

Today's waterfowlers have access to vastly improved outerwear and other gear compared with hunters of that era, but too many still know little about protecting themselves from weather and staying comfortable in a marsh. Many hunters have simply learned to adjust to a certain degree of discomfort while in the field, remaining content with a comfort level that is merely tolerable. By definition, if you are not uncomfortable, you are comfortable. If an excess of heat, cold, or moisture makes us uncomfortable, then minimizing those effects will make us comfortable. Sounds simple, but given the elements that face most duck hunters throughout the season, comfort is easier to define than it is to achieve.

Since it is not uncommon for a person to lose more than a quart of water per hour during heavy exertion—lugging decoys into a swamp qualifies as heavy exertion—the ideal clothing for waterfowling keeps rain and snow out while letting sweat evaporate. Developing a waterproof garment that was also breathable once seemed about as feasible as making a perpetual motion machine—at least until the birth of Gore-Tex™ in 1976. This waterproof, breathable membrane has been the most revolutionary advancement in hunting gear since the

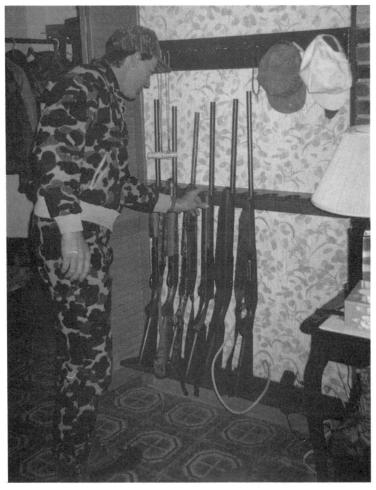

Space-age technology has revolutionized sporting wear. Compared to waterfowling clothes of yesteryear, modern garments are warmer, lighter, and less bulky. Photo by Chris Dorsey.

advent of camouflage. Some early Gore-Tex garments had problems with leakage, but it wasn't the membrane itself that was leaking, but the seams where sewing needles perforated the Gore-Tex fabric. Advances in seam-sealing techniques largely remedied this fault. Despite early glitches, Gore-Tex has become the standard in waterproof and breathable fabrics. Contrary to common belief, W. L. Gore and Associates—manufacturers of Gore-Tex—doesn't actually make clothing or boots, but scores of manufacturing partners use Gore-Tex fabric in their products.

Since the advent of Gore-Tex, several companies have begun marketing clothing advertised as both waterproof and breathable— Sympatex, Microtec, Entrant, Omni-Tech, and Ultrex, to name a few. The questions are, just how waterproof and just how breathable? A wide range of waterfowling gear is made from these fabrics and laminates, and you don't necessarily have to purchase the most expensive items to achieve satisfactory performance.

Too many hunters end up purchasing garments advertised as water repellent, but then discover firsthand the difference between water *repellent* and water*proof.* Waterproof garments should withstand water entry even in active use. For example, when kneeling, a 165-pound person exerts about 16 pounds per square inch on the knee area of the garment. Though some pants advertised as waterproof might keep you dry while you are standing, the moment you add pressure—such as

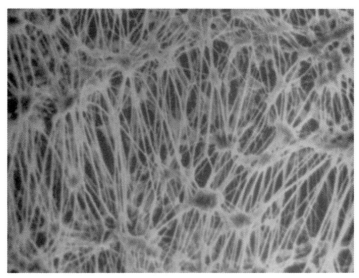

This is a microscopic look at Gore-Tex membrane. It has some nine billion pores per square inch, allowing perspiration vapor to pass through without letting water penetrate. The membrane is now used in a wide variety of garments worn by sportsmen. Courtesy W.L. Gore & Associates.

when kneeling—they may leak. If you are looking for quality water-fowling gear that will serve you well in rigorous use, avoid garments that are merely water repellent and stick to waterproof clothing.

DRESSING LIKE A DUCK

Before the advent of space-age fibers and materials, a waterfowler stayed warm and dry in the blind by wearing a cotton shirt and a wool or down jacket, topped with a rubber coat. If he wanted his clothing to breathe, he opened the jacket and let in the air.

Though wool and down are both marvelous insulating materials when dry, when wet they lose much of their insulating quality as the air space between the fibers fills with water. Polyester and polypropylene each absorb less than 0.5 percent of their weight in water, but cotton absorbs 8 percent and wool 17 percent. It's the dead air space in a garment that gives it its insulating qualities, and these modern synthetic fibers don't absorb moisture as readily as do their natural counterparts.

Whether you are a modernist or traditionalist in your choice of waterfowling gear, it's a good idea to follow old but sensible advice: dress in layers. Start with an undergarment that wicks perspiration from your skin, like polypropylene, polyester, or silk. Typically, the farther away from your skin you move moisture, the warmer you'll be, since the spaces between the fibers nearest your body will be filled with air instead of water.

When hunting in cold conditions, consider wearing a cotton or fleece layer over this, followed by a breathable, windproof, waterproof insulated jacket. Increase the thickness of insulation based on how active you plan to be. If you will be rowing, paddling, or poling your way across a marsh, be sure to wear another wicking layer over your polypropylene or silk undergarments, for you'll need fabrics that will keep perspiration from soaking the area around your skin. Conversely, if you are planning on little activity while hunting during cold weather, you'll need added insulation.

Conservation author Chuck Petrie and his Lab Gunnar prepare for a day of diver hunting in northern Wisconsin. Dressing for comfort includes wearing a coat that is both waterproof and breathable. Photo by Chris Dorsey.

Decoy designer Darrel Wise (left) and Minnesota guide Pete Carlson collect the spoils of the day.
The Backland camo they are wearing is the creation of waterfowler Scott Anderson. Photo by
Chris Dorsey.

Don't be bashful about trying on clothes at a sporting goods
store. Don a jacket, zip it up all the way, and test your mobility. Walk
over to the gun counter and ask to look at a gun. Try mounting the gun
to your shoulder while both sitting and standing. Does the jacket allow you enough range of motion to shoot effectively? With the hood
up, can you see in a wide field of view, or is your peripheral vision
blocked? When you turn your head left or right, does the hood move
with you or stay stationary, blocking your view? Are the pockets deep
enough to hold enough shells without letting them fall out? Does the

camouflage pattern of the coat match the cover you typically hunt? With so many camo patterns on the market today, it has never been easier to blend into your surroundings.

Waterfowlers often overlook their feet, hands, and head when purchasing hunting garments, but it is from these areas that some 80 percent of body heat is lost. Finding gloves that are waterproof, breathable, warm, and not too bulky to wear while shooting is still remarkably difficult—even as we approach the twenty-first century. As a left-handed shooter, I now wear one heavily insulated glove on my right hand and a leather shooting glove on my trigger hand. It's not ideal, but I'd rather sacrifice some warmth for the added dexterity— especially when a brace of mallards is hovering over my decoys.

Gore-Tex hats and booties lined with Thinsulate insulation are essentials for cold-weather waterfowling. Don a pair of silk or polypropylene socks and pull the booties over them before inserting your feet into a pair of insulated pack boots, and your stay in the cold confines of a late-season blind will be far more comfortable. It's important not to forget the wicking layer on your feet; there are some fifteen hundred sweat ducts on each foot, and each day an average pair of feet gives off a pint and a half of perspiration. When it comes to selecting footwear for hunting, John DePalma of Irish Setter Sport Boots offers the following tips:

1. Select a properly fitted boot; cramped toes will eventually weaken the foot. In 1992, Americans spent more than $26 billion to help cure foot ills. The difference between a shoe size (9 to 10, for instance) is only a third of an inch.

2. To break in a stiff pair of hiking or hunting boots, wet them completely inside and out and walk them dry.

3. Never dry a wet boot by direct heat or sunlight; that will shrink the leather.

4. To accelerate the drying of a wet boot, stuff it full of newspapers.

5. If you plan to purchase boots from a store, buy them at the end of the day when your feet are swollen.

World champion duck caller Tim Gesch blends well with his surroundings using Backland camouflage, a remarkably versatile pattern for waterfowlers. Photo by Chris Dorsey.

6. Carry a fanny pack with a second pair of socks, and change your socks frequently. This will help keep your feet warmer when it's cold.

7. Remove inserts (insoles) from boots at the end of the day to help speed drying.

8. Wool socks are superb choices for outdoor wear. Wool absorbs perspiration and cushions the foot.

THE AGE OF NEOPRENE

Few advancements in waterfowling gear have been more welcome than neoprene waders. While plenty of people continue to buy and use the bulky rubber-and-canvas waders of yesteryear, a growing number of waterfowlers—especially those who hunt frequently in cold weather—are discovering the virtues of neoprene.

The introduction of neoprene has forever altered the definition of comfort in the marsh. The insulating qualities of neoprene waders make them a favorite choice of waterfowlers who frequent cold environs. Photo by Chris Dorsey.

The most noticeable advantage of neoprene is warmth. Neoprene's cellular structure traps a lot of air; the thicker the neoprene the greater the insulating value (common thicknesses range from 3 to 5 millimeters). This layer of waterproof insulation will keep your keister dry when you sit on a muskrat hut or stumble and fall in a marsh. Neoprenes also tend to be much more formfitting than their conventional counterparts, making it far easier to maneuver about a brushy slough or flooded timber bottom.

Neoprene also is less susceptible to ultraviolet damage and dry rot than are other wader materials. Nothing's perfect, however, and neoprene waders are more prone to puncturing than rubber and nylon waders. Many manufacturers have overcome this problem by covering the neoprene with a puncture-resistant coating. Early models were prone to seam leakage, but with improved seam-sealing technology, this problem has been solved.

No matter the wader material, most duck hunters prefer waders with integral boots. Boot-foot waders trap less mud and decaying vegetation than do stocking-foot waders with separate overboots, and they're usually warmer, since they contain more dead air around the foot. Lug soles can be a tremendous aid in negotiating greasy marsh bottoms. In streams or rivers with rocky bottoms, the felt-soled boots favored by trout anglers increase traction on slippery rocks.

For many cold-weather waterfowlers, neoprene waders have forever redefined comfort in the duck marsh. Indeed, returning to the old rubber waders after testing a pair of neoprenes seems a bit like surrendering your favorite shotgun to duck-hunt with a bow and arrow.

BINOCULARS FOR THE BLIND

There are as many sound reasons to carry a pair of binoculars into the blind with you as there are species in the marsh. Not only can you enjoy spying on wildlife up close, but you'll be able to identify ducks before you shoot at them. The death of the point system—where each species of duck had its own point value used to determine the daily bag limit—didn't change the fact that you still need to identify ducks on the wing before you pull the trigger.

A great way to practice waterfowl identification is to play "name that species," using your naked eye, as ducks fly by in the distance. When you think you've made an accurate identification, raise your binoculars to see if you were correct. By continually quizzing yourself, you'll quickly improve your ability to identify ducks and geese on the wing. And don't reserve this practice just for the hunting season; spring migration provides the perfect excuse to get back in the marsh and practice both your duck calling and waterfowl identification.

When choosing binoculars for waterfowling, a model that provides an ample field of view will enable you to track the sometimes erratic path of birds in flight. Since ducks and geese are most active in the low-light periods of morning and evening, you'll need binoculars that maximize available light. Finally, select binoculars that are both waterproof and durable; eventually they'll be dropped in a boat, submerged when wading, or chewed on by a formerly favorite retriever.

Too many hunters overestimate the importance of power and underestimate the benefit of field of view. Power refers to the ability to magnify objects in the distance—the number of times larger an object will appear when viewed through the binoculars compared with the naked eye. A pair of 8× binoculars, for instance, will magnify an object eight times. Though increased power makes an object appear closer, it does so at the expense of field of view. With a wide field of view, you'll be able to locate an object more quickly.

Equally important is brightness—the amount of light needed to see an object clearly with a given pair of binoculars. The common misconception is that low-power binoculars are brighter than high-power models, but this simply isn't true. The measure of a binocular's brightness derives mostly from the size of the exit pupil—the small disk of light visible in the eyepiece when the binoculars are held at arm's length and pointed toward the sky or a bright light.

The typical human pupil expands to about 6 or 7 millimeters under low-light conditions. Any exit pupil smaller than that transmits less light than the pupil can use. For the optimum configuration—an exit pupil as close as possible to 6 to 7 millimeters—the objective lens (the largest lens of any optic) should be six or seven times larger than the optic's power. Dividing the objective lens diameter in millimeters by the magnification will give you the exit pupil's diameter. A 10×40mm pair of binoculars, for example, has an exit pupil of 4.

Then there's the decision between compact or full-sized binoculars. While the smaller optics have the obvious advantage of portability, their exit pupil is often too small to view wildlife for extended periods without eyestrain. Furthermore, compact binoculars generally have neither the light-gathering capability nor the field of view found in full-size binoculars.

Choosing optics is a balancing act, weighing the advantages and disadvantages of each model against your needs. The more you know about them, the easier it will be to choose the correct pair of binoculars.

X

Where Waterfowling is Celebrated

There are a few communities in America where, at least for a brief period each year, local residents won't look at you funny if you practice blowing a feed chuckle while walking down Main Street. In these towns, waterfowling traditions run deep, and the birds, and the hunters who pay homage to them each autumn, enjoy the same reverence normally reserved for special holidays. Five such towns include Easton, Maryland; Reelfoot, Tennessee; Stuttgart, Arkansas; Pointe Mouillee, Michigan; and St. Charles, Illinois.

EASTON, MARYLAND

The Easton Waterfowl Festival owes its origins to a 1971 newspaper story by local columnist Bill Perry, suggesting that Easton establish an event to celebrate the area's rich waterfowl resource. Dr. Harry Walsh soon joined Perry's cause, and together the pair convinced the Talbot County chapter of Ducks Unlimited that a waterfowl festival would benefit both the birds and the community. Since then, the Easton Waterfowl Festival has been an annual event on the second weekend in November, raising nearly $3 million for waterfowl conservation.

The festival, which is held prior to the annual goose-hunting season, has thrived despite recent declines in local goose populations. The Eastern Shore of Maryland was once legendary for its unsurpassed

WILD GOOSE.

Illustration from Field Sports of the United States and British Provinces, *1848.*

goose hunting but, because of several successive cold springs on Quebec's Ungava Peninsula—the breeding area for the Atlantic population of Canada geese—goose numbers declined throughout the 1980s. Hunters on the Eastern Shore once enjoyed a ninety-day season with a three-goose-per-day limit. By the early 1990s, the season and limit had been cut to a fraction of that.

While hunters still travel to Easton before the annual goose season to enjoy the festival, thousands of others flock to the quaint community simply to enjoy the event's many art displays, shows, and waterfowling demonstrations. The annual Federal Duck Stamp is unveiled during the festival, and the World Championship Goose Calling Contest is also held there. While today's version of the festival has more to do with wildlife art than waterfowling, there remains plenty to keep even the most ardent waterfowler entertained.

Visitors of the annual Waterfowl Festival held in Easton, Maryland, can witness, among other attractions, the World Goose Calling Championship. Photo by Chris Dorsey.

SANBURG (REELFOOT), TENNESSEE

Since 1990, Sanburg, Tennessee, has hosted the annual Reelfoot Lake Call Makers and Collectors Waterfowl Festival. Those attending will find more than six hundred feet of display frontage under canopy along the shores of Reelfoot Lake, a region with the distinction of being the cradle of American duck calling. A large assortment of call and decoy collectibles are bought and sold at the event, which is held the second weekend in August each year. Additional wildlife exhibits, a retriever show, and even a slingshot exhibition are some of the many events held during the festival.

Judges at the World Goose Calling Championship in Easton, Maryland, listen to contestants from across North America compete for the coveted title. Photo by Chris Dorsey.

STUTTGART, ARKANSAS

Few towns enjoy the notoriety among waterfowlers of Stuttgart, home of the World Championship Duck Calling Contest. While many duck hunters from across the nation hope one day to stand on that stage in Stuttgart, few will succeed. The first duck calling contest was held here prior to World War II, and the contest has since grown to incorporate

The annual Michigan Duck Hunters Tournament, held near Monroe, features a wide variety of contests including layout and sneakbox shooting. Photo by Jerry Warrington.

many events in addition to the calling championship. It has become known as the Wings over the Prairie Festival, more reflective of its expanded offerings.

The Queen Mallard Pageant is yet another featured attraction, drawing scores of the region's most beautiful young women to compete. A dinner and dance add a festive flair, and few who attend miss either the Duck Gumbo Cookoff or the Fun Shoot. In past years, entertainment has included such showstoppers as the Dallas Cowboy Cheerleaders. Art fairs and shows featuring sporting collectibles are also mainstays. The Wings over the Prairie Festival is traditionally held the week of Thanksgiving, and usually precedes the earliest Arkansas duck season.

MONROE (POINTE MOUILLEE), MICHIGAN

The annual Michigan Duck Hunters Tournament is perhaps the most unusual of all such events held around the country, packed as it is with such contests as sneak shooting, layout shooting, punt-boat racing, rowing race, duckboat rowing race, hip-boot marsh race, and marsh shooting championship.

There are also regional duck and goose calling contests, retriever trials, decoy and other art shows, a trading post, raffles, children's events, and many others. The tournament has been in existence nearly fifty years, and was founded by "Hy" Dahlka, a legendary waterfowling figure from the region. Proceeds from the event are used to improve the Pointe Mouillee Marsh, located fifteen miles north of Monroe, a town that proudly proclaims itself the Hometown of General George Custer. The Michigan Duck Hunters Tournament is held each September.

ST. CHARLES, ILLINOIS

If collecting old waterfowling paraphernalia is your fancy, you'll want to be in St. Charles, Illinois, the last weekend in April, for the nation's largest decoy show. Gene Konopasek, president of the Midwest Decoy Collectors Association, the group sponsoring the event, says the show is held "after tax season and before fishing season each year." The event dates back to 1964, when the first group of collectors assembled to sell and trade their wares. Participants now can peruse more than four hundred tables full of sporting collectibles, including decoys, calls, books, art, boats, and many other items.

XI

Ducks Unlimited:
A Conservation Original

For many, the name Ducks Unlimited invokes images of a dinner banquet rife with tales of past northeasters delivering gifts of migrating ducks. Some are reminded of Terry Redlin sunsets, prints that recall the simple pleasures of country life. Others hear DU and think of the Lab pup that, with one lick on the cheek, won its way into a family's hearts. Still others joke that, if it weren't for DU, they might have enough cash left to buy a box of steel 2s.

The engine of the organization is fueled by all those individuals, hunters who feel compelled to give something back to the environment from which they derive so much satisfaction. It is from first-hand visits to the marshlands that these waterfowlers have come to understand the value of such places—not only to wildlife, but also to themselves.

This concern was the genesis of Ducks Unlimited, a conservation organization that arose from the Dust Bouel days of the 1930s to champion the cause of wetland preservation. The progenitor of Ducks Unlimited was the Game Conservation Society, which merged with the More Game Birds in America Foundation, a group begun by New York philanthropist and printing magnate Joseph Palmer Knapp. If any one person can be called the father of Ducks Unlimited, it is Knapp, for he devoted much of his considerable wealth, vision, and energy to launching the organization. Perhaps the most important achievement

Ducks Unlimited projects throughout North America provide essential breeding, migratory, and wintering habitat for a myriad of waterfowl species. Photo by Scott Nielson, courtesy Ducks Unlimited, Inc.

of More Game Birds was its landmark 1935 International Wild Duck Census, the forerunner of surveys still conducted today.

Ducks Unlimited was incorporated in 1937 from the merger of the Game Conservation Society with the More Game Birds in America Foundation, and within a year some 6,720 supporters had raised $90,000 for wetland conservation efforts. Data from the 1935 Wild Duck Census had made it clear that, for duck hunting in America to improve, critical wetland habitat on the Canadian breeding grounds must be secured. In 1938, Ducks Unlimited Canada was formed, the biological and engineering affiliate of Ducks Unlimited Inc. Money raised in the United States by DU Inc. went north to fund habitat work on the important waterfowl breeding grounds.

Manitoba's Big Grass Marsh was once a lush, 100,000-acre wetland that drained nearly 1,000 square miles and was the breeding ground of countless waterfowl. To most local residents and to the Manitoba government, however, this marsh was an impediment to the provinces' future prosperity. In 1910, the Manitoba North Western

More Game Birds in America busily published books and pamphlets to document the status of North American wildfowl and to help show sportsmen how they could improve conditions for duck and geese.

THE 1935 INTERNATIONAL WILD DUCK CENSUS

A REPORT ON THE DUCK POPULATION IN ALBERTA, SASKATCHEWAN, MANITOBA, NORTH DAKOTA, SOUTH DAKOTA AND MINNESOTA DURING AUGUST, 1935.

MORE GAME BIRDS IN AMERICA

A FOUNDATION

500 FIFTH AVENUE   NEW YORK CITY

The project was undertaken by the More Game Birds in America Foundation in 1935. The organization was the forerunner of Ducks Unlimited. Courtesy Ducks Unlimited Archives.

Participants in the first ever International Wild Duck Census pose for a photo in front of one of the planes used for the count.

Drainage Company began to channelize and drain Big Grass Marsh. What followed was a man-made environmental catastrophe of un-precedented magnitude. Wells ran dry throughout the area. Livestock withered under the drought of the 1930s, and foreclosures began to swallow farm after farm. As the water left the marsh, so did life.

In 1938, with much local fanfare, Ducks Unlimited undertook the resurrection of Big Grass Marsh, constructing a number of dams to halt the wetland's loss of water. Four years later, the marsh had returned to near-normal water levels, completing the organization's first project. Since then, Ducks Unlimited has conserved roughly 7 million acres of

This series of photos illustrates the plight of Manitoba's Big Grass Marsh, the site of the first Ducks Unlimited project. The top photo (opposite page) was taken in 1906, before the marsh was drained.

Big Grass not only served as a major recreational area, it supplied water for agriculture in the region, provided thousands of acres of wildlife habitat, and stored water to recharge groundwater aquifers. Despite such benefits, the Manitoba North Western Drainage Company, with the blessing of the provincial government, began work to drain the marsh in 1910. It didn't take long for the marsh and area wells to sun dry, creating an environmental catastrophe unlike any previously seen in the region. In 1938, ducks Unlimited began work to resurrect the marsh, which included damming the canals previously dug to drain the wetland. Courtesy Ducks Unlimited Archives.

important waterfowl habitat across Canada, the United States, and Mexico. With affiliate organizations in all three countries, Ducks Unlimited can address the needs of migrating wildfowl, which live for a time in each country on their journey between breeding and wintering grounds.

Today, Ducks Unlimited has more than 500,000 members across the United States. While DU remains focused on North American wildfowl, it has exported its expertise to other nations with similar organizations, helping them develop their own conservation plans and

Ducks Unlimited used this powerful photo to illustrate the plight of North American ducks during the decade-long drought of the 1980s. The drought crippled duck production across the prairies of Canada and the Dakotas and led to some of the lowest duck populations in 30 years. Courtesy Ducks Unlimited Archives.

funding sources. EuroDucks and Ducks Unlimited New Zealand are two examples of Ducks Unlimited's worldwide influence. DU programs in Denmark, South Africa, and Argentina have also been explored.

Since its inception, Ducks Unlimited has raised more than $800 million, drawing on its nationwide network of more than 3,000 chapters, which sponsor special events that raise nearly $40 million each year. Increasingly, major corporations are earmarking large sums to DU and the cause of wetlands conservation.

The late Bing Crosby made regular appearances on "The American Sportsman," ABC's Emmy-award winning outdoors program hosted by Curt Gowdy. The pair frequently advanced the cause of waterfowl conservation, helping Ducks Unlimited spread the message of wetland preservation to a national audience. Courtesy Ducks Unlimited Archives.

In addition to its work in Canada and Mexico, Ducks Unlimited's Matching Aid to Restore States Habitat (MARSH) program has conserved nearly 1 million acres of habitat, with projects in every U.S. state. Regional DU offices in Bismarck, North Dakota; Sacramento, California; and Jackson, Mississippi, have led to scores of partnerships with both public and private organizations to save existing wetlands or to create new habitat.

Through its Washington, D.C., office, Ducks Unlimited's staff closely monitors key legislation that might affect the future of wetlands and waterfowl. By providing policymakers with sound biological information about the myriad benefits of wise land stewardship, DU encourages management approaches that leave room for wildlife.

Perhaps the most important piece of legislation to affect wildlife conservation in recent history was the Conservation Reserve Program,

By returning bands recovered on ducks and geese, thousands of hunters across the hemisphere helped wildlife biologists map the flyways used by North American waterfowl. Photo by Chuck Petrie.

Susie and her charge—may they always have a home. Photo by Scott Nielsen, courtesy Ducks Unlimited, Inc.

part of the 1985 Farm Bill. Farmers were paid to take cropland out of production, with the stipulation that the land must lay idle for ten years. Since the program's inception, nearly 40 million acres of marginal farmland across the country have been set aside and planted to grassy cover. Though the program was designed to reduce soil erosion and boost commodity prices, the benefits to wildlife, such as upland birds and grassland-nesting waterfowl, were unprecedented. Recognizing the importance of this program to waterfowl, Ducks Unlimited's considerable resources are targeted toward ensuring its continuation.

There are many fronts to the fight for wetland conservation, each as important as the other. While hands-on habitat work is central to the organization's efforts, failure to monitor legislation affecting wildlife could negate decades of concerted work. Educating people about the many virtues—both aesthetic and financial—of wetlands is yet another challenge facing Ducks Unlimited.

Enjoy the festive atmosphere of a Ducks Unlimited banquet but remember that an enormous challenge lies ahead for DU volunteers and staff, for resurrecting waning waterfowl populations has much in common with moving mountains.

XII

A Look Ahead

Sometimes when retracing the byways of my youth, I find it difficult to remain optimistic about the future of wildlife and hunting. Many of the marshes that were both classrooms and companions during my formative years have fallen to those who see wetlands merely as a place to grow crops or mortgages, heedless of the cumulative impact when that becomes collective community doctrine. For it isn't the draining of a single wetland that poses the greatest challenge to wildlife, but the belief that it is acceptable to do so.

Advocating wetland preservation based solely on its benefits to waterfowlers is selfish. The value of wetlands is in their uniqueness, for they are, ultimately, a link in the great chain that sustains life on our planet. In practical terms, wetlands are the environment's sponges. When we remove these environs, we are, in effect, canceling nature's flood insurance. With 80 percent of the Mississippi River's bottom-lands already gone, it's no surprise that residents along that river's course have been inundated by an ever-increasing number of floods once thought of as hundred-year occurrences.

Wetlands also help purify our water, filtering out the many agricultural and residential chemicals and poisons that find their way to our water systems. By holding water on the land, wetlands help recharge overused—in some parts of the country, decimated—underground aquifers, the sole source of drinking water for thousands of

CROW AND HEN REDHEAD.

Illustration from The Ducks Came Back, *1945.*

communities in rural America. For many species of wildlife, no ecosystem is as important as wetlands. Some 43 percent of America's threatened or endangered plant and animal species rely on wetlands at some point in their life cycles.

Some who might abhor the leveling of a mountain wouldn't blink at the loss of a wetland, yet placing a higher value on one or the other is to suppose either is replaceable. If history has shown us anything about man's effect on the land, it is that efforts to improve nature and natural systems often make matters worse. As biologist Richard McCabe wrote, "It appears now that the first concern is not so much a matter of creating cover as of preventing its destruction."

There is, at last, a growing recognition that wetlands can no longer be viewed through a pioneer's eyes as impediments to growth and prosperity, to turn away from the unfortunate human trait of seeing little value in things—whether passenger pigeons, wilderness, or wetlands—until they are lost forever. Even our short-sighted politi-

With over half of America's wetlands already gone, work to halt marshland destruction has never been more vital to the future of wildfowl. Photo by Scott Nielsen, courtesy Ducks Unlimited, Inc.

If the potholes of Western Canada and the Dakotas are dry, many prairie nesting species will fly north until they find water. Clutch size, however, tends to be smaller when ducks that normally nest on the prairies bypass the area for northern regions. Photo by Scott Nielsen, courtesy Ducks Unlimited, Inc.

cians have belatedly turned their attention to slowing the loss of wetlands. But with some 53 percent of America's wetlands already gone—
more than 90 percent in states like California—one can only wonder
how many more acres will be sacrificed before the assault is stopped.

The 1985 Food Security Act, otherwise known as The Farm Bill,
featured conservation provisions that were among the strongest in history. While America's wildlife have often suffered under agricultural
policy, this bill's Conservation Reserve Program took marginal farm-
lands out of production, creating nearly 40 million acres of upland
cover across America, much of it in the plains states, to the great benefit of scores of nesting ducks, pheasants, prairie grouse, and other
game and nongame species. This linkage between conservation pro-

Blue-winged teal are one of several prairie nesting species that suffered heavy losses during the drought of the 1980s.
When the rains returned, refilling the potholes in the mid 1990s, however, the birds demonstrated how fast they
could rebound. Photo by Scott Nielsen, courtesy Ducks Unlimited, Inc.

Biologists used a nasal saddle to mark this blue-winged teal hen during a reproductive study conducted in Wisconsin. Waterfowl research has been critically important in developing management schemes to help bolster duck populations. Photo by Chuck Petrie.

grams and agricultural policies is something of an environmental epiphany. Seventy percent of our nation's ducks breed on private land—predominantly farmland.

The precipitous decline of ducks throughout the 1980s—largely the result of a prolonged drought across the Prairie Pothole Country of western Canada and the Dakotas, an area that produces three out of every four ducks found in North America—revived a sense of urgency among conservationists across the continent. The result was the North American Waterfowl Management Plan, the blueprint experts hope will eventually return duck populations to 1970s levels, when some 100 million ducks filled autumn skies from the Yukon-Kuskokwim Delta to Laguna Madre.

Research has shown that predatory rates on duck nests are lower on the large tracts of retired farmland associated with the Conservation Reserve Program than they are on smaller islands of cover common to Waterfowl Production Areas. Such information has helped wildlife managers to realize some of the many benefits of the CRP. Photo by Scott Nielsen, courtesy Ducks Unlimited, Inc.

The NAWMP's objectives of improving and protecting 28 million acres of habitat at a cost of $6 billion by 2025 make it one of the most ambitious wildlife restoration efforts ever undertaken. The plan is also significant in that it is a joint effort between public and private sectors in three nations: Canada, America, and Mexico. Since many North American waterfowl species rely on habitat in each country to sustain them on their annual migrations, a serious effort to restore continental duck populations must involve habitat conservation in each nation. Having breeding grounds in Canada, for instance, is fruitless if the birds have no place to rest and recharge their fat reserves in winter. Beware of quick-fix solutions and gimmicks in waterfowl conservation, for no task this daunting is completed without great toil and dedication.

The underlying long-term dilemma facing not just waterfowl but all wildlife is the increased pressure being placed on habitat by a growing human population. As cities and suburbs expand, more water, minerals, and land are needed to sustain them. Although

The mallard expansion into traditional black duck breeding range has resulted in an increasing rate of hybridization between the two species. Photo by Scott Nielsen, courtesy Ducks Unlimited, Inc.

America's population growth has been relatively stable compared with that of other nations, our population has doubled since World War II, and demand for land, water, and other resources has grown at an exponential rate.

While duck populations have been declining, most goose species have actually made significant gains. Geese nest in the far north, away from major human influences by man, and at no time in history have there been more birds. Resident goose populations also continue to expand in several states, in some cases to the point of becoming nuisances on golf courses and in residential areas.

Not surprisingly, the number of duck and goose hunters is linked to the number of ducks and geese, a correlation that becomes clear when comparing a chart of duck populations with that of the sales of duck stamps. For example, in 1970, Federal Duck Stamp sales reached a peak of 2.4 million at the same time that spring duck breeding counts approached a near-record high of almost 40 million birds. By 1990, breeding populations had plummeted to 25 million birds, and the

Despite unprecedented efforts by hunters to preserve wetland habitat, the fate of these important ecosystems remains in jeopardy as threats from development increase with our growing human population. Photo by Chris Dorsey.

number of waterfowlers subsequently declined to 1.3 million. Water-fowlers have historically been our greatest advocates of wetland and wildlife conservation, with contributions that extend far beyond dollars. Any nationwide groundswell of support for wetlands preservation must ultimately begin with sportsmen.

So we are left with a spirit of both optimism and of trepidation about the future of wildfowl. Pressure continues to grow on wetlands and other ecosystems upon which ducks and geese depend, but programs such as the CRP may become a mainstay of American agricultural policy, expanding both habitat and hope for North American ducks and geese. If efforts to create a similar program in Canada succeed, the goal of 100 million ducks may become a reality. Work on the NAWMP will further help the situation, and individual commitment will continue to be the cornerstone of future conservation efforts, for nothing can be achieved without the will of the people.

XIII

*W*aterfowl on the Table

An old waterfowling salt once told me that the toughest part of goose hunting was finding someone who wanted the birds he had shot. Comments like that reflect the age-old practice of cooking waterfowl well done. For those who have learned to savor medium-rare duck and goose, a well-done bird is an over-done bird.

Unless well-done wildfowl is prevented from dehydrating during cooking, the meat can be about as appetizing as tough old liver. There's a limit to the abilities of sauces, marinades, and plum jelly to resurrect poorly cooked duck or goose.

Nonetheless, well-done duck and goose *can* be delicious. Savvy chefs have long used moisture-imparting fruit or vegetable stuffings to prevent dehydration during cooking. Cooking the birds in foil or an oven bag to trap additional moisture helps too. For best results, cook slowly at a low temperature for several hours until the meat falls from the bone.

If well-done fowl is not your fancy, there are innumerable crowd-pleasing ways to prepare medium to rare duck or goose. Some of the best goose I've ever tasted, for instance, came from the grill of a camp along Hudson Bay. Seared over high heat and served rare in thin slices, the meat more closely resembled prime beef filet than a goose breast. Some may feel, however, that rare fowl is too radical a culinary departure.

BLUEBILL DRAKES—THEIR FAMILY DUTIES ARE OVER.

Illustration from The Ducks Came Back, *1945.*

Others feel the key to preparing duck or goose is making them taste like something other than what they are. For those not fond of wildfowl's trademark robust flavor, there is the old practice of marinating, which helps tenderize the meat and improve its taste. A general rule when marinating game is, the older and gamier the meat, the stronger the marinade and the longer it should marinate. The lighter the color of the duck or goose, the less you will want to marinate it, for light-colored meat will be more tender and less gamey tasting than birds with very dark flesh.

Tenderness and flavor depend not only on age, but also vary according to species and recent diet. Many Louisiana restaurants used to serve mergansers, the fishy-tasting flesh of which is served as an inexpensive alternative to fish in seafood gumbo. Diving ducks dine primarily on animal life and tend to be stronger flavored than primarily vegetarian puddle ducks. Some people prefer the stronger-tasting divers, although this may be due more to a general reverence for diver hunting than to culinary interest.

No matter the fowl, there is a wine to complement it. Generally, robust red wines go best with the hearty flavor of wildfowl. Most reds are at their best if left at room temperature and opened at least half an hour before serving. Most whites are served chilled, and need not breathe before being served. When planning an elaborate duck or goose dinner, you will want a succession of wines that refresh the palate with each course.

Here is a wine guide from California chef Michael-Jan Regules that will help you in planning your next wildfowl dinner:

THE WINE LIST

To prepare a sweet sauce—such as cranberry, lingonberry, chutney, or orange—for a duck or venison dish, I highly recommend a *Zinfandel*, a uniquely American wine. The character of Zinfandel does not overpower the sweet harmony of such dishes. Here are three Zinfandels I have found to be excellent:

Bannister 1992 Dry Creek
Gabrielli 1992 Mendocino
Ridge Geyserville 1991 Sonoma

For a herbaceous or savory sauce accompaniment, consider a *Pinot Noir* or a *Merlot*. Both harmonize well with such sauces. My favorites include:

Ridge California Greenwood 1993 Pinot Noir
Santa Cruz Mountain Vineyard 1990 Pinot Noir
Camelot 1993 Santa Barbara Pinot Noir
Shaffer 1992 Napa Valley Merlot
Stags Leap 1991 Napa Valley Merlot

Vintage Choices

The first rule of modern wine tasting is that there are no hard and fast rules. The notion that only red wines should be served with red meat and only white wine with poultry and fish is as antiquated as the wooden decoy. Dining on duck or goose without a fine wine is like hunting without a gun. Wine stimulates appetite, aids conversation, and improves digestion. And certain substances in red wine are said to act as Drano for the arteries, keeping them clear despite heavy fat consumption. The French are living proof of wine's medicinal qualities, for their diets contain large amounts of fat, yet they suffer less heart disease than fat-conscious Americans.

From Swamp to Soup: Cleaning Wildfowl

There are several ways to prepare ducks and geese for the table, but none as time-honored as dry plucking. Commercially available pluckers range from elaborate models that cost several hundred dollars to portable drill attachments that run about the price of three boxes of steel duck loads. Of course, many people prefer to pluck ducks the old fashioned way: with thumb, index finger, and elbow grease.

I recall hunting with a few old-timers who liked to pluck their ducks in the blind. For them, it was a way to pass the time between flights, like whittling on a piece of wood. Unfortunately, the down and feathers on the bottom of the blind always seemed to find a way to blow up my nose and stick to anything wet—like retrievers, guns, and shells.

Rather than make the area surrounding my blind look like a chicken processing plant, I usually pluck the breast, back, and wing feathers in a nearby field. When I get home, I dip the bird in melted paraffin

(cont'd. next page)

RECIPES TO DIE FOR

One of the best parts of traveling across the globe in search of waterfowling is tasting the many sumptuous ways ducks and geese can be prepared. The following recipes have brought countless hours of dining pleasure to people from South Carolina to South Africa. They are culinary gems, one and all.

Hutchison Island Dream Duck with Currant Sauce

Buddy Kronsberg, Hutchison Island Duck Club, South Carolina

> *4 mallard-sized ducks, plucked*
>
> *2 medium oranges*
>
> *2 medium apples*
>
> *2 medium onions*
>
> *½-pound thick bacon*
>
> *6-ounce jar currant jelly*
>
> *½-stick butter*
>
> *Lawry's Seasoning Salt*
>
> *Worcestershire sauce*
>
> *cinnamon*
>
> *pepper*

Pat plucked ducks dry with paper towel. Salt and pepper cavities. In this order, stuff each with ½ orange, ½ onion, and ½ apple. Generously coat birds with Lawry's Seasoning Salt. Place bacon strips over breasts. Place each bird on aluminum-foil, breast up; wrap loosely and crimp closed on top. Place wrapped birds together on cookie sheet and slow-roast at 250 degrees for 6 hours. Serve with currant sauce. In saucepan, empty jar of currant jelly, add ½-stick butter, and cinnamon and Worcestershire sauce to taste. Heat until boiling and spoon over ducks. Serve with appetizers of either shrimp cocktail or oysters on the half shell, followed by the main course of duck with long-grain white rice, mixed greens, and a dessert of pecan pie or peach ice cream. Serves four.

*   *   *

Tendele Duck à l'Orange

Chef Camilla Comins, Tendele Lodge, South Africa

4 plucked mallards

1 cup chicken stock

3 tablespoons sugar

3 tablespoons red wine vinegar

3 tablespoons fresh-squeezed orange juice

2 tablespoons Grand Marnier

2 teaspoons grated orange rind

cornstarch

Fillet duck breasts from bone, leaving skin on. Place breasts on tray and bake at 500 degrees for 7 to 10 minutes or until medium rare. Slice breasts diagonally and thin. To prepare sauce, caramelize sugar, then add vinegar, orange juice, Grand Marnier, and grated orange rind. Keep over heat and add chicken stock; thicken with cornstarch. Spoon sauce over sliced duck and serve with red cabbage, snap peas, and wild rice. Serves four.

* * *

Duck Breasts with Black and Mahogany (brown) Rice and Chutney Sauce

Chef Michael-Jan Regules, Can Can Club, Suisun, California

16 ounces cooked black and mahogany rice (wild rice can be substituted)

4 duck breasts

salt

pepper

all-purpose flour

4 ounces Major Grey or homemade chutney (mild and fruity)

2 tablespoons unsalted butter

1½ tablespoons hazelnut, almond, or peanut oil

½ cup demi-glace or brown sauce (can be made fresh or packaged Knorr Swiss demi-glace)

(cont'd. next page)

From Swamp to Soup: Cleaning Wildfowl
(cont'd.)

and simply peel off the waxed down. The fastidious can remove the few remaining pinfeathers with a pair of tweezers. This is purely cosmetic, however, for the skin is retained primarily to prevent the meat from drying out during roasting; most people don't eat it. Keep in mind, though, that if you plan to transport birds across state or international lines, or from field to home, by law you may need to leave a wing, head, or both intact so that law enforcement personnel can identify the species.

Once the bird is plucked, make a small incision between the bottom of the breast and the vent. From here, the bird can be drawn using your thumb and forefinger. You can remove the head either with the stroke of an ax or by using a knife, cutting between the joints unless you want to spend more time sharpening your blade than you did cleaning your bird. Next, rinse the bird under cold water to wash off excess blood and any loose feathers, and it's ready for the

(cont'd. next page)

**From Swamp to Soup:
Cleaning Wildfowl**
(cont'd.)

oven or the freezer. Be
sure birds intended for the
freezer are well wrapped.
A friend of mine removes
air from the package with
a vacuum sealer, and has
few problems with freezer
burn.

For recipes calling for duck
or goose breast fillets, you
won't even need to pluck
your fowl. Simply peel
back the skin over the
breast to expose the
meat, then cut along the
breast bone and around
the breast plate, just as in
deboning a chicken. When
finished you'll be left with
two breast-meat
medallions; on mallard-
sized ducks, each will be
about the size of a large
deck of cards. This method
takes less time and effort
than plucking, and breast
fillets occupy little space in
the freezer.

2 tablespoons finely chopped shallots

Combine:

1 tablespoon Balsamic vinegar

½ cup Zinfandel

¼ cup port

¼ cup plum wine

Season both sides of duck breasts with salt and pepper. Dust lightly with flour.
Heat large, heavy skillet over moderate heat. Place oil and 2 tablespoons butter in skillet. When skillet is hot, place breasts skin-side down for about 3 minutes. Turn to other side for an additional 3 minutes of cooking or until done
medium rare. Breasts should be golden brown. Remove breasts and place aside
on plate. Pour off any excess fat from the pan, add shallots and combined
wines and vinegar. Let liquid deglaze the skillet, then add demi-glace. Allow
the mixture to reduce by half. Add chutney and simmer for about 2 minutes.
Place 4-ounce portion of rice on each plate, position breast atop rice, and
spoon sauce over duck breast. Serve with steamed asparagus and cranberries.
Serves four.

*   *   *

Melted Goose with Plum Sauce
Mary Petrie, Fence Lake, Wisconsin

poultry seasoning

1 large goose, plucked

1 apple

1 onion

1 orange

1 30-ounce can purple plums (whole)

1½ cups pineapple juice

½ cup brandy

½ cup brown sugar

3 tablespoons cornstarch

(cont'd. next page)

1 teaspoon cinnamon

1 teaspoon cloves

cayenne pepper

salt

Clean goose cavity and pat dry. Rub poultry seasoning in cavity and sprinkle with salt. Stuff cavity with quartered apple, onion, and orange. Place goose in covered roasting pan and roast slowly in 250-degree oven for approximately 4½ hours until tender. Baste every 20 minutes after goose has been in oven for one hour. To make perfect plum sauce, drain plums and save juice. In saucepan, mix juice from plums, brandy, pineapple juice, butter, and spices. Cook over medium heat, stirring constantly. Bring to boil and add cornstarch. Reduce heat and stir until thickened. Add plums, stir until plums are thoroughly heated and spoon over goose. Serve with green beans, cranberries, and wild rice. Serves four.

*   *   *

Sky Carp Cajun Sausage

Terry Shaughnessy, Hackberry Rod & Gun, Hackberry, Louisiana

3 pounds goose breast fillets

4 pounds pork shoulder

½ pound pork fat

2 tablespoons salt

1 tablespoon pepper

1 teaspoon garlic powder

½ teaspoon allspice

¼ teaspoon nutmeg

½ minced onion

Cajun Seasoning

Chunk meat and grind coarsely. Combine seasonings and mix with meat. Grind again to mix thoroughly and stuff sausage skins. Cut in 1-inch thick diagonal slices, lightly sprinkle Cajun Seasonings over pieces, and fry until completely cooked. Compliments any breakfast menu.

*   *   *

Fired-up Goose
Pam DeLong, New Matamoras, Ohio

> 6 snow goose breast fillets
>
> 1 cup Worcestershire sauce
>
> 1 cup red wine
>
> 1 cup teriyaki marinade
>
> ½ cup soy sauce
>
> 2 pressed garlic cloves

Mix ingredients and marinate breasts for 12 hours, turning every hour. Grill over hot coals until medium rare. Serve with cranberries, wild rice, and acorn squash. Serves six.

*   *   *

Chicken-Fried Goose Strips
Peggy Sherrill, W. S. Sherrill Waterfowling Club, Wharton, Texas

> 2 goose breast fillets
>
> flour or cracker meal
>
> 2 beaten eggs
>
> Tony Chachere's Creole Seasoning
>
> cooking oil

Slice goose fillets across grain into ½-inch wide strips. Season to taste with Tony Chachere's Creole Seasoning or your favorite seasonings. Dip seasoned strips in egg and coat with flour or crushed saltines. Heat small amount of cooking oil in a heavy skillet until very hot. Fry strips, turning repeatedly until cooked thoroughly. Serve with scalloped potatoes, green salad, garlic bread, and a dessert of fresh peach cobbler. Serves four.

*   *   *

References

Allen, Durward L., *Our Wildlife Legacy*, Funk & Wagnalls, New York, NY, 1962.

Atwill, Lionell, *Sporting Clays—An Orvis Guide*, Atlantic Monthly Press, New York, NY, 1990.

Aziz, Laurel, *Decoys*, Camden House Publishing, Camden East, Ontario, Canada, 1994.

Back Then, Willow Creek Press, Wautoma, WI, 1989.

Baldassarre, Guy A., *Waterfowl Ecology and Management*, John Wiley & Sons, New York, NY, 1994.

Barber, Joel, *Wild Fowl Decoys*, Dover Publications, New York, NY, 1954.

Begbie, Eric, ed., *Modern Wildfowling*, Saiga Publishing Co., Surrey, England, 1980.

———, *The New Wildfowler*, Stanley Paul and Co., London, England, 1989.

Bellrose, Frank, *Ducks, Geese & Swans of North America*, Stackpole Books, Harrisburg, PA, 1978.

———, *Ecology and Management of the Wood Duck*, Stackpole Books, Harrisburg, PA, 1994.

Blacklock, Craig, *The Geese of Silver Lake*, Voyageur Press, Stillwater, MN, 1989.

Bodio, Stephen, *Good Guns*, Nick Lyons Books, New York, NY, 1986.

Boyd, Hugh et. al., *Duck Wings*, Harrison Zoological Museum, Kent, England, 1975.

Bruette, William, *American Duck, Goose & Brant Shooting*, Howard Watt Publisher, New York, NY, 1929.

Bush, Walter L., *A Saga of Duck & Goose Hunting*, American Wildlife Galleries, Minneapolis, MN, 1978.

Cadieux, Charles L., *Goose Hunting*, Stone Wall Press, Boston, MA, 1979.

Carlson, Delbert, *Dog Owner's Home Veterinary Handbook*, Howell Book House, New York, NY, 1992.

Choate, Ernest A., *The Dictionary of American Bird Names*, Harvard Common Press, Boston, MA, 1985.

Coykendall, Ralph, Jr., *Duck Decoys and How To Rig Them*, Winchester Press, Piscataway, NJ, 1983.

DiSilvestro, Robert L., *The Endangered Kingdom*, John Wiley & Sons, New York, NY, 1989.

Ducks Unlimited Continental Conservation Plan, Ducks Unlimited, Memphis, TN, 1994.

Dudley, Jack, *Carteret Waterfowl Heritage*, Decoy Magazine, Morehead City, NC, 1993.

Duffy, Trent, *The Vanishing Wetlands*, Impact Books, New York, NY, 1994.

Dunning, Joan, *Secrets of the Nest*, Houghton-Mifflin, New York, NY, 1994.

Fergus, Charles, *Gun Dog Breeds*, Lyons & Burford Publishers, New York, NY, 1993.

Fleckenstein, Henry A., Jr., *American Factory Decoys*, Schiffler Publishing, Exton, PA, 1981.

Fleming, Patricia, ed., *Traditions in Wood*, Camden House Publishing, Camden East, Ontario, Canada, 1987.

Gibbons, Boyd, *The Retriever Game*, Stackpole Books, Harrisburg, PA, 1992.

Gresham, Grits, *The Complete Wildfowler*, Stoeger Publishing Co., South Hackensack, NJ, 1973.

Grinnell, George B., *American Duck Shooting*, Stackpole Books, Harrisburg, PA, 1991.

Hammer, Donald A., *Creating Freshwater Wetlands*, Lewis Publishers, Chelsea, MI, 1992.

Harlan, Howard, *Duck Calls*, Harlan-Anderson Press, Nashville, TN, 1988.

Hazelton, William, ed., *Supreme Duck Stories*, Gunnerman Press, Auburn Hills, MI, 1989.

Hinman, Bob, *The Duck Hunter's Handbook*, Winchester Press, Piscataway, NJ, 1985.

Hochbaum, H. A., *Wings Over the Prairie*, Tamos Books, Winnipeg, Canada, 1994.

Johnsgard, Paul A., *Waterfowl*, University of Nebraska Press, Lincoln, NE, 1968.

Johnson, Archie, *Gun Clubs & Decoys of Back Bay & Currituck Sound*, CarBac Press, Virginia Beach, VA, 1991.

Kimball, David and Jim, *The Market Hunter*, Dillon Press, Minneapolis, MN, 1969.

Lacy, Ann T., *Perdew—An Illinois River Tradition*, Boyce Forms Systems, Muncie, IN, 1993.

Leffingwell, William B., *Shooting on Upland, Marsh, and Stream*, Rand, McNally & Co., New York, NY, 1890.

Lendt, David L., *The Life of Jay Norwood Darling*, Iowa State University Press, Ames, IA, 1989.

Lewis, Fielding, *Tales of a Louisiana Duck Hunter*, Vantage Press, New York, NY, 1988.

Linn, John R., *Finding the Extra Target*, Shotgun Sports, Auburn, CA, 1989.

Lucky, Carl F., *Collecting Antique Bird Decoys and Duck Calls*, Books Americana, Florence, AL, 1992.

Mackey, William J., Jr., *American Bird Decoys*, Dutton, New York, NY, 1965.

MacQuarrie, Gordon, *Stories of the Old Duck Hunters*, Willow Creek Press, Minocqua, WI, 1994.

Madge, Steve, *Waterfowl*, Houghton Mifflin Co., Boston, MA, 1988.

Martin, Laura C., *The Folklore of Birds*, Globe Pequot Press, Old Saybrook, CT, 1993.

Miller, Stephen, *Early American Waterfowling 1700s–1930*, Winchester Press, Piscataway, NY, 1986.

Milner, Robert, *Retriever Training for the Duck Hunter*, Safari Press, Long Beach, CA, 1985.

Mitchell, John G., *The Hunt*, Alfred A. Knopf, New York, NY, 1980.

Pearce, Michael, *Sporting Clays*, Stackpole Books, Harrisburg, PA, 1991.

Peterson, Harold L., *The Remington Historical Treasury of American Guns*, Rutledge Books, New York, NY, 1966.

Pough, Richard H., *Audubon Water Bird Guide*, Doubleday & Company, Garden City, NY, 1951.

Reiger, George, *The Wings of Dawn*, Stein and Day Publishers, New York, NY, 1980.

Roberts, Kenneth G., *The Canoe*, Macmillan of Canada, Toronto, Canada, 1983.

Schroeder, Robert, *Wildfowl Carving*, Stackpole Books, Harrisburg, PA, 1992.

Short, Lester, *The Lives of Birds*, Henry Holt, New York, NY, 1993.

Stroud, Richard H., *National Leaders of American Conservation*, Smithsonian Institution Press, Washington, D.C., 1985.

Stewart, Jim, *Decoys of a Thousand Islands*, The Boston Mills Press, Erin, Ontario, 1991.

Tarrant, Bill, *Problem Gun Dogs*, Stackpole Books, Harrisburg, PA, 1992.

Taylor, Zack, *Customizing Small Boats*, Winchester Press, Tulsa, OK, 1981.

———, *Successful Waterfowling*, Stackpole Books, Harrisburg, PA, 1974.

Tennyson, Jon et. al., *Canvasbacks of Minnedosa*, Delta Station Press, Manitoba, 1991.

Walsh, Roy E., *Gunning the Chesapeake*, Tidewater Publishers, Centreville, MD, 1960.

Webster, David S., *Decoys at Shelburne Museum*, Shelburne Museum, Shelburne, VT, 1961.

Weller, Milton W., *Freshwater Marshes*, University of Minnesota Press, Minneapolis, MN, 1994.

Wentz, Richard, ed., *Return to Big Grass*, Ducks Unlimited Inc., Long Grove, IL, 1986.

Wesley, David E., ed., *Fireside Waterfowler*, Stackpole Books, Harrisburg, PA, 1987.

Wilson, R.L., *Winchester—An American Legend*, Random House, New York, NY, 1991.

Wolters, Richard A., *Duck Dogs*, Dutton, New York, NY, 1990.

Zutz, Don, *Shotgun Stuff*, Shotgun Sports, Auburn, CA, 1991.

———, *Shotgunning Trends in Transition*, Wolfe Publishing Co., Prescott, AZ, 1989.

I n d e x